FE Lecturer's Guide to Diversity and Inclusion

Other titles in The Essential FE Toolkit Series

Books for lecturers

Teaching the FE Curriculum – Mark Weyers

e-Learning in FE – John Whalley, Theresa Welch and Lee Williamson

FE Lecturer's Survival Guide – Angela Steward

How to Manage Stress in FE – Elizabeth Hartney

Guide to Teaching 14–19 – James Ogunleye

Ultimate FE Lecturer's Handbook – Ros Clow and Trevor Dawn

A to Z of Teaching in FE – Angela Steward

Getting the Buggers Motivated in FE – Sue Wallace

Books for managers

Everything You Need to Know About FE Policy – Yvonne Hillier

Middle Management in FE – Ann Briggs

Managing Higher Education in Colleges – Gareth Parry, Anne Thompson and Penny Blackie

Survival Guide for College Managers and Leaders – David Collins

Guide to Leadership and Governance in FE – Adrian Perry

Guide to Financial Management in FE – Julian Gravatt

Guide to Race Equality in FE – Beulah Ainley

Ultimate FE Leadership and Management Handbook – Jill Jameson and Ian McNay

A to Z for Every Manager in FE – Susan Wallace and Jonathan Gravells

Guide to VET – Christopher Winch and Terry Hyland

FE Lecturer's Guide to Diversity and Inclusion

Anne-Marie Wright,
Sue Colquhoun, Jane Speare,
Sina Abdi-Jama
and Tracey Partridge

continuum

Continuum International Publishing Group

The Tower Building   80 Maiden Lane, Suite 704
11 York Road   New York
London   NY 10038
SE1 7NX

British Library Cataloguing-in-Publication Data
A catalogue record for this book is available from the British Library.

ISBN: 0 8264 8844 7 (hardback)

Library of Congress Cataloging-in-Publication Data
A catalog record for this book is available from the Library of Congress.

Typeset by YHT Ltd
Printed and bound in Great Britain by MPG Books Ltd, Bodmin, Cornwall

Contents

Dedication

This book is dedicated to our colleague and friend Sina Abdi-Jama who contributed two important chapters to the *FE Lecturer's Guide to Diversity and Inclusion*, but has not lived to see its publication.

Sina came to Manchester from Somalia at an early age and was brought up in a strong, self-respecting and generous family. From this experience emerged a mature woman. Sina was sure of her traditions, faith and culture, and within these made independent choices. She enjoyed marriage to Mahamood, their daughters Hana and Aneesa, study and employment and she made her mark in a varied career in education. Sina worked in schools, colleges, and professional development and latterly at the University of Greenwich. Her empathy and focus was principally with refugee and ESOL learners but she modelled good practice with a sureness and integrity that spoke to all.

Inside and outside the classroom Sina combined honesty with compassion and her courage was liberally sprinkled with humour.

Although only having about half the time on earth that we in the West sometimes casually expect, Sina's was a life fully lived. She engaged with and enriched the lives of her family, colleagues, friends and students. She will continue to do so through our memories.

Thank you Sina.

Series foreword

THE ESSENTIAL FE TOOLKIT SERIES

Jill Jameson
Series Editor

In the autumn of 1974, a young woman newly arrived from Africa landed in Devon to embark on a new life in England. Having travelled half way round the world, she still longed for sunny Zimbabwe. Not sure what career to follow, she took a part-time job teaching EFL to Finnish students. Having enjoyed this, she studied thereafter for a PGCE at the University of Nottingham in Ted Wragg's Education Department. After teaching in secondary schools, she returned to university in Cambridge, and, after graduating, took a job in ILEA in 1984 in adult education. She loved it: there was something about adult education that woke her up, made her feel fully alive, newly aware of all the lifelong learning journeys being followed by so many students and staff around her. The adult community centre she worked in was a joyful place for diverse multiethnic communities. Everyone was cared for, including 90-year-olds in wheelchairs, toddlers in the crèche, ESOL refugees, city accountants in business suits and university level graphic design students. In her eyes, the centre was an educational ideal, a remarkable place in which, gradually, everyone was helped to learn to be who they wanted to be. This was the Chequer Centre, Finsbury, EC1, the 'red house', as her daughter saw it, toddling in from the crèche. And so began the story of a long interest in further education that was to last for many years . . . why, if they did such good work for so many, were FE centres so under-funded and unrecognized, so underappreciated?

It is with delight that, 32 years after the above story began, I write the Foreword to *The Essential FE Toolkit*, Continuum's new series of 24 books on further education (FE) for teachers and college leaders. The idea behind the *Toolkit* is to provide a comprehensive guide to FE in a series of compact, readable books. The suite of 24 individual books are gathered together to provide the practitioner with an overall FE toolkit in specialist, fact-filled volumes designed to be easily accessible, written by experts with significant knowledge and experience in their individual fields. All of the authors have in-depth understanding of further education. But 'Why is further education important? Why does it merit a whole series to be written about it?' you may ask.

At the Association of Colleges Annual Conference in 2005, in a humorous speech to college principals, John Brennan said that, whereas in 1995 further education was a 'political backwater', by 2005 it had become 'mainstream'. John recalled that since 1995 there had been '36 separate Government or Government-sponsored reports or white papers specifically devoted to the post-16 sector'. In our recent regional research report (2006) for the Learning and Skills Development Agency, my co-author Yvonne Hillier and I noted that it was no longer 'raining policy' in FE, as we had described earlier (Hillier and Jameson, 2003): there is now a torrent of new initiatives. We thought in 2003 that an umbrella would suffice to protect you. We'd now recommend buying a boat to navigate these choppy waters, as it looks as if John Brennan's 'mainstream' FE, combined with a tidal wave of government policies will soon lead to a flood of new interest in the sector, rather than end anytime soon.

There are good reasons for all this government attention on further education. In 2004/2005, student numbers in LSC-funded further education increased to 4.2m, total college income was around £6.1 billion, and the average college had an annual turnover of £15m. Further education has rapidly increased in national significance regarding the need for ever greater achievements in UK education and skills training for millions of learners, providing qualifications and workforce training to feed a UK national economy hungrily in competition with other OECD nations. The 120 recommendations of the Foster Review (2005) therefore in the main encourage colleges to focus their work on vocational skills, social inclusion and achieving academic progress. This series is here to consider all three of these areas and more.

The series is written for teaching practitioners, leaders and managers in the 572 FE/LSC-funded institutions in the UK, including FE colleges, adult education and sixth form institutions, prison education departments, training and workforce development units, local education authorities and community agencies. The series is also written for PGCE/Cert Ed/City & Guilds Initial and continuing professional development (CPD) teacher trainees in universities in the UK, USA, Canada, Australia, New Zealand and beyond. It will also be of interest to staff in the 600 Jobcentre Plus providers in the UK and to many private training organisations. All may find this series of use and interest in learning about FE educational practice in the 24 different areas of these specialist books from experts in the field.

Our use of this somewhat fuzzy term 'practitioners' includes staff in the FE/LSC-funded sector who engage in professional practice in governance, leadership, management, teaching, training, financial and administration services, student support services, ICT and MIS technical support, librarianship, learning resources, marketing, research and development, nursery and crèche services, community and business support, transport and estates management. It is also intended to include staff in a host of other FE services including work-related training, catering, outreach and specialist health, diagnostic additional learning support, pastoral and religious support for students. Updating staff in professional practice is critically important at a time of such continuing radical policy-driven change, and we are pleased to contribute to this nationally and internationally.

We are also privileged to have an exceptional range of authors writing for the series. Many of our series authors are renowned for their work in further education, having worked in the sector for thirty years or more. Some have received OBE or CBE honours, professorships, fellowships and awards for contributions they have made to further education. All have demonstrated a commitment to FE that makes their books come alive with a kind of wise guidance for the reader. Sometimes this is tinged with world-weariness, sometimes with sympathy, humour or excitement. Sometimes the books are just plain clever or a fascinating read, to guide practitioners of the future who will read these works. Together, the books make up a considerable portfolio of assets for you to take with you through your journeys in further education. We hope the experience of reading the books will be interesting, instructive and pleasurable and that experience gained from them will last, renewed, for many seasons.

It has been wonderful to work with all of the authors and with Continuum's UK Education Publisher, Alexandra Webster, on this series. The exhilarating opportunity of developing such a comprehensive toolkit of books probably comes once in a lifetime, if at all. I am privileged to have had this rare opportunity, and I thank the publishers, authors and other contributors to the series for making these books come to life with their fantastic contributions to FE.

Dr Jill Jameson
Series Editor
March, 2006

Series introduction

FE Lecturer's Guide to Diversity and Inclusion – **Anne-Marie Wright, Sue Colquhoun, Jane Speare, Sina Abdi-Jama and Tracey Partridge**
This book is dedicated to Sina Abdi-Jama, one of the co-authors for this thoughtful, sensitive and valuable book, the *FE Lecturer's Guide to Diversity and Inclusion*. It provides a fitting testament to Sina's work in post-compulsory education and training at the University of Greenwich and to her earlier years in schools, colleges and professional development.

At the point in time we agreed the book proposal, we did not realize quite how ill Sina was. Typically generous, positive, and self possessed, Sina chose to focus on what she could do for others, rather than her illness. Her passing was a great shock and source of sad loss to many. We remember and honour Sina for her kindness, generosity, excellent work and sensitive understanding of the complex issues outlined in this *Guide to Diversity and Inclusion*. The book lives on to celebrate Sina Abdi-Jama's name, her family, and all of her many achievements.

The *FE Lecturer's Guide to Diversity and Inclusion* presents a collection of specialist chapters for FE lecturers, including both an academic overview of theoretical knowledge in this field and practical suggestions for implementation in the classroom. Concepts of 'difference', 'diversity' and 'inclusive education' are explored by the authors within the context of an overall framework for reflection on 'difference' to encourage positive attitudes about the diverse challenges facing FE lecturers. The book aims to enable FE lecturers to develop inclusive classrooms within inclusive colleges, for the benefit of both students and staff.

There is an extraordinary range and diversity of learners in the FE system: in Chapter 1, this book provides an overall introductory theoretical and practical overview of diversity and inclusion issues that affect many of this very large number of students. Chapter 2 focuses on 'English for speakers of other languages' (ESOL), outlining the current context of the *Skills for Life* initiative and highlighting the importance of valuing multilingualism to support the many different groups of ESOL learners in the UK.

The complex, challenging needs of refugee students in post compulsory education, and the difficulties of teaching and assisting this group of learners, with suggestions for supporting teachers themselves, provide the focus for Chapter 3. Chapter 4 discusses the roles of teaching support staff, providing guidelines for the professional appointment, effective employment and evaluation of this invaluable group of staff. Chapter 5 outlines the difference between sex and gender, giving an overview of differences in participation and achievement of males and females, summarising the context for sex discrimination legislation and promoting a range of strategies to challenge gender inequalities. Chapter 6 gives an overview of the role of emotions in learning, demonstrating how emotions affect behaviours and attitudes in the classroom, comparing behavioural with psychodynamic approaches and offering alternative strategies for behaviour management. Chapter 7 concerns younger learners in FE, notably 14 to 16 year olds: it encourages lecturers to adopt a positive and constructive mindset to this group, outlining strategies to help lecturers provide a good learning environment for younger learners. Chapter 8 considers issues of dyslexia, providing clinical information on the symptoms and diagnosis of dyslexia, supplemented by practical strategies for lecturers to teach dyslexic students in an inclusive culture. Chapter 9 provides information about autism and Asperger's syndrome, including diagnostic, clinical and psychological theory, with expert reflections from the authors. The chapter outlines characteristic behaviours of this group of learners, explaining the neurology of autism to inform and support lecturers.

This excellent book on diversity and inclusion in FE is informed by the many years' experience of our expert post-compulsory education authors' team. It is a 'must-read' for FE lecturers, trainee lecturers, teaching support staff, managers, policy makers, trainers and a range of other personnel wishing to promote an inclusive, diverse culture within inclusive classrooms and colleges across the UK and internationally. I recommend it most highly to you, with thanks to Anne-Marie, Sue, Jane and Tracey, and in remembrance of Sina.

Dr Jill Jameson
Director of Research
School of Education and Training
University of Greenwich
j.jameson@gre.ac.uk

Introduction

At the time of writing, the authors of this book are working as senior lecturers in the Department of Post-compulsory Education and Training (PCET) at the University of Greenwich, London, the largest provider of initial and in service further education lecturer/teacher training (FETT) in the UK. The authors have all previously worked as lecturers and departmental managers in general further education (FE) colleges in the London area and, collectively, have many years of experience 'at the chalk face' in the PCET sector and, more recently, in preparing new lecturers for work in the sector.

It is our experience that in the early days of training, when a new lecturer begins to learn the skills to teach and to manage learning and assessment, he or she usually understandably views the students as a homogeneous group and plans learning outcomes for the whole class to achieve. Very quickly it becomes apparent that this strategy is not enough – the trainee lecturer is introduced to the concept of 'differentiation', and so begins the task of writing group profiles, collating individual learning plans and becoming vigilant about how well each individual is engaging and performing.

For the authors of this book, who have spent their professional lives in and around FE colleges, the challenge of meeting the needs of individual students, whose previous experience of learning and education may have been less than positive, is the essence of teaching in the FE sector and brings the greatest reward. Enthusiasm to provide a more positive and rewarding educational experience for such students is something we actively set out to inspire in our trainee lecturers, although most of them come to training with this commitment and understanding having already taken seed in their hearts and minds. It becomes our job to then provide them with some skills in understanding how difference works in classrooms and how differentiated learning can be delivered.

Getting to know each student in a class, understanding what each person already knows, how he or she learns and taking the time to understand the intrinsic or extrinsic barriers to learning already experienced is a significant challenge to new lecturers, but one which must be overcome if their teaching is to make a difference. We hope you find this book informative and helpful and that, most of all, it dispels some of your uncertainty about the overused mantra of 'differentiation'.

This book presents a collection of chapters which primarily provide trainee lecturers and lecturers new to FE with some skills about how to manage individual learning needs and individual differences in mainstream classrooms. Each chapter combines an academic context for the topic and some practical guidelines for inclusion.

Chapter 1 begins by exploring the concepts of 'difference' and 'diversity' through the emerging paradigm of inclusive education. It provides a framework for thinking about difference and for developing a positive attitude to the challenges students bring to FE classrooms. It offers some practical ideas about some of the ways lecturers can work to develop inclusive classrooms within inclusive colleges.

Chapter 2, 'English for Speakers of Other Languages' (ESOL), aims to capture the range and diversity of learners encountered in FE and sets out to define some of the many terms used. It touches on the history of immigration to the UK and illustrates the ways in which theories of bilingualism and second language acquisition have evolved, locating ESOL within the current context of the Skills for Life initiative. Of central importance is the underlying imperative to value multilingualism as a means of securing a sense of personal and political belonging for ESOL learners who may well feel isolated from the dominant culture in the UK. The chapter concludes by recommending practical strategies and approaches for achieving this within the FE classroom.

Chapter 3 looks at the needs of refugee students in post-compulsory settings. Trauma can manifest itself in a number of ways in the classroom, but we counsel the most effective way for teachers to react. It also describes the support that should be forthcoming for those teachers working under 'intense' conditions.

Chapter 4 focuses on the support staff who are present in post-compulsory settings. It looks at ways of managing support and ensuring clarity with regards to maintaining professionalism. It also highlights the need to evaluate that support and avoid dependency.

Chapter 5 considers gender, clarifies the distinction between sex and gender and illustrates the ways in which education can either challenge or perpetuate traditional sexist stereotypes. It outlines the differences in participation and achievement between males and females, starting at school and continuing through various aspects of adult life. A brief historical background provides the context for the legislation governing sexual discrimination, against which current practice is discussed. The chapter concludes by considering a range of strategies aimed at challenging gender inequalities within vocational education based on practical projects that have been implemented in various institutions within the post-compulsory sector.

Chapter 6 examines the role of emotions in learning and how the emotional experience of teaching and learning can affect the behaviours and attitudes of teachers and students. The chapter invites teachers to think about their own emotions and those of their students in order to understand and make sense of difficult behaviours in the classroom and to respond constructively to them rather than react emotionally. It contrasts behavioural approaches with psychodynamic thinking and offers alternative strategies for teachers in their approach to behaviour management.

Chapter 7 is about younger learners in further education. The chapter acknowledges the negative perceptions that some FE lecturers may have about working with 14–16-year-olds and supports readers in thinking about these learners in a positive and constructive way. It invites lecturers to consider the experience of FE from the point of view of the younger learner as well as from their own vantage points, to confront their concerns, and to ask the right questions about how these learners can be positively included in the wider context of teaching in FE. It provides a range of useful and practical strategies for thinking and for providing a learning experience that both values and includes younger students.

Chapter 8 considers the issue of dyslexia. It offers some clinical information about symptoms and diagnosis through an exploration of the history of dyslexia in education. It offers many practical strategies for lecturers engaged in teaching dyslexic students and advocates dyslexia-friendly methods as part of a whole-college approach in an inclusive culture.

Chapter 9 offers some information about autism and Asperger's syndrome. It provides some diagnostic information and a brief discussion of the clinical and psychological aspects of these associated conditions. It then explores some of the behaviours that students who are on the autistic spectrum may present. Most importantly, by explaining the neurology of autism in 'layman's' terms, the chapter sets out to dispel the myths surrounding autism and Asperger's syndrome and to support the lecturer in developing positive and confident attitudes to teaching autistic students in mainstream settings.

This book is intended to be a beginning. The authors hope you enjoy the book, as each chapter represents our individual area of interest, research and expertise, which we have developed over time by engaging with continuous professional development in our field. We do not intend this book to represent all there is to know about diversity. We acknowledge that we have not dealt with mental health, deafness, blindness or physical disability. That is not because we do not think that these are important, merely that our own particular expertise did not stretch that far. So there is more to read and to research.

1 Inclusion: The new discourse for diversity?

The law is an expression of the will of the community. All citizens have a right to concur, either personally or by their representatives, in its formation. It should be the same to all, whether it protects or punishes; and all being equal in its sight are equally eligible to all honours, places and employments, according to their different abilities, without any other distinction than that created by their virtues and talents.

Paine, *The Rights of Man*, 1772, the Sixth Right

The chapters of this book offer ideas and teaching tips for how to manage difference in classrooms through an understanding of what inclusive education means in practice. The key to creating inclusive classrooms is providing differentiated learning in a culture in which learners are equally valued, and yet the concept of differentiation remains a constant challenge for even the most experienced teachers. For trainee teachers and newly qualified teachers, differentiation is perhaps the last thing with which they grapple after learning aims, outcomes and assessment have all been confidently understood. Differentiation is about planning and assessing learning that meets the requirements of the curriculum and also takes account of cognitive abilities, learning-style preferences and an array of other individual needs. To ensure every learner is valued, included and reaches his or her potential for achievement and progression, in a context in which learners have very diverse needs is, by anybody's estimation, a tall order!

What is inclusive education?

Inclusive education is concerned with all learners and can be understood as an ideology which invites schools and colleges to appraise their cultures and value systems and to judge their effectiveness by how well they offer every learner a way to succeed and progress, regardless of their ability, gender, age, language, ethnic or cultural origin (Thomas and Loxley 2001, p. 119).

The development of inclusive education as part of a socially just, diverse and democratic society represents the latest, and perhaps most robust, challenge to the long-standing, seemingly immovable orthodoxy of segregated and selective education in this country. Inclusive education offers a new way to negotiate the impasse of selection for unequal provision which has dominated the evolution of our education system for the last century (Whitty 2002, p. 128).

In offering equality of opportunity, barrier-free learning and widened participation and integration, inclusive education is not a short-term, 'bolt on' initiative to solve an immediate social or educational problem associated with one group of learners. In other words, it is not simply about how learners with special needs are provided for, or how well colleges reach out to their local communities to include those who may be socially and educationally marginalized. Although these individuals are at the heart of inclusive educational thinking, to conceptualize inclusive education in this reductionist way is to misunderstand its essence. Inclusive education is an ideology that challenges colleges to find ways to measure how well they respond to diversity and inequality, and to assess how genuinely they invite and welcome all members of their local community to learning as equal participants and with an equal right to belong. It requires colleges to be creative in finding ways to measure these values, as opposed to valuing only those things that can be easily measured.

The origins of inclusive education

'Inclusion' as an ideology emerged in the early 1990s and superseded the previous notion of 'integration'. The essential difference between inclusion and integration is that 'integration' is a product, an end result, whereas inclusion is a process and a means to an end. Integration describes the setting where learners with special or additional needs are placed to learn, i.e. in a classroom, a unit or a resource base. It also carries an implicit expectation that learners need to change, and preferably improve, in order to be ready to enter the mainstream of a college.

Inclusion is very different. Inclusion requires the institution to change and not the learner. In inclusive settings, the learner is intrinsically valued and accepted and it is the institution that must change its policies, structures and curricula if these restrict access or present any barrier to full participation by the learner. Most importantly, in inclusive settings learners who may be judged to be 'different' are not segregated, marginalized or regarded as needing special attention or provision; they are part of the mainstream learning community and are free to make choices and to find their place within the curriculum and to access the support they may need without unnecessary exposure to 'specialist' professionals, systems or assessments.

In further education colleges, this means that learners choose courses to meet their interests and needs and are not restricted by grouping or selection according to ability, gender, disability, sexuality, race, religion or ethnic origin (Thomas and Vaughan 2004, p. 134). Inclusion means the end of 'discrete' courses designed for those with physical disabilities or sensory impairments, or those who may have mental health needs or emotional and behavioural difficulties. In inclusive colleges, *what* a learner wants and needs to learn becomes the priority, not how, where or with whom he or she should learn it.

'Inclusive education is an unabashed announcement, a public and political declaration and celebration of difference. It requires continual proactive responsiveness to foster an inclusive educational culture.' (Corbett and Slee 2000, p. 134)

Human rights

> 'Inclusive thinking has developed through political and social frameworks in which the discourse has changed from segregation, categorisation, need and authority, to one of rights, participation and social justice and of greater democracy, fraternity and equity.' (Thomas and Vaughan 2004, p. 3)

In this country, one of the main drivers of inclusive education has been the Centre for Studies in Inclusive Education (CSIE) which in 1989 launched a charter for inclusion to work towards an end of segregation in education on the grounds of disability or learning difficulty (Thomas and Vaughan 2004, p. 135). The ideology underpinning the CSIE's work is a belief that inclusive education is 'comparable to equality as a social value in relating to all aspects of social disadvantage, oppression and discrimination' (Lunt and Norwich 1999, p. 23).

In 1994, the United Nations Educational, Scientific and Cultural Organization (UNESCO) world conference held in Salamanca, Spain produced a declaration which 64 countries, including the UK, signed. The declaration called upon all world governments to 'adopt as a matter of law or policy the principles of inclusive education' (UNESCO 1994). The 'Salamanca Statement' formed the basis for the government's Green Paper, 'Excellence for All' (1997) which set out a strategy for inclusive education supported and influenced by the Disability Rights Task Force's report 'From Exclusion to Inclusion' published in 1999.

It is difficult to extricate all the influences that converged around the end of the twenty-first century to result in a demand for more inclusive practice in all sectors of education. In the USA, the inclusion movement had gathered pace, and in the UK, lobbyists who had been separately representing the interests of people with disabilities and pupils with learning difficulties began to speak with one voice and were finally heard.

The social model of disability

The thinking which connected, and still connects, groups such as The Disability Rights Commission (DRC) and the CSIE is an advocacy for more equitable and just political, social and education systems. This thinking is ideologically rooted in what is known as 'the social model of disability', which is based on the belief that disability and special educational needs are created by the way society is organized in its perpetuation of disabling environments and promotion of hostile social attitudes (Barnes 1996, p. 43). Moreover, the social model of disability does not lie within the individual. Rather, it is a social construction imposed by a society which designs itself on a physically and intellectually 'perfect' norm. The social model shifts the focus from what was known as the 'medical model' which was concerned with 'diagnosing' what might make the individual 'different' and then developing a 'prescription' for what might be needed to support him or her to perform to the 'norm'. The social model understands that civilized communities have a collective responsibility for making society and all its constructs accessible and available to all. The social model of disability is underpinned by three pivotal beliefs:

1. the way those who are disabled are talked about, categorized and labelled creates a culture of need (Corbett 1996; Ware 1995)
2. society's institutions (in this case schools/colleges) create failure by segregating and selecting students (Ainscow 1997)
3. the ways in which society organizes itself (by class and social capital) marginalizes and disadvantages certain groups (Barnes 1996; Barton 1988; Oliver 1988; Tomlinson 1982, 1985, cited in Clark, Dyson and Millward 1998, p. 158).

The Special Educational Needs and Disability Act

The British Government consulted widely following Salamanca and responded to the findings with the Special Education

Needs and Disability Act 2001 (SENDA), which amended both the Disability Discrimination Act and the 1996 Education Act. SENDA has finally provided the foundation from which true inclusive education can now be built.

SENDA has two parts:

Part 1 amends the 1996 Education Act and describes the duty on the education system to educate disabled children in ordinary schools, governed by two provisos or caveats:

1. that it is in accordance with the parents' wishes; and
2. that it does not affect the efficient education of other children.

Part 2 amends the Disability Discrimination Act 1995 (DDA), which came into force in September 2002 and covers access issues in all sectors of education. SENDA makes it unlawful to discriminate against a disabled person in admission arrangements, provision of education and associated services or by exclusions. It also calls for increased accessibility in terms of the curriculum, the physical environment and information (SENDA 2001).

SENDA promotes the idea that all 'disabled' students have equal rights to benefit from and contribute to the learning and services available in educational institutions. SENDA requires that providers be proactive in totally removing barriers to learning and participation, not just in improving access, but also in promoting inclusive admissions policies and curricula tailored to meet a broader range of needs.

Inclusion in schools is currently the subject of a contentious and fiercely fought debate between those who are unequivocally in favour of the closure of all special schools and those who argue with equal passion for a child's right to be educated separately if his or her needs demand it (Farrell 2001; Mittler 2000).

Inclusive learning: the Tomlinson Report

Inclusion in the context of FE is arguably considerably less contentious than in schools, but is still not fully understood.

The notion of inclusive education first entered FE in 1996 through the publication of *Inclusive Learning* (Tomlinson 1996). The Tomlinson Report, as it was known, was ground breaking and in its way was far ahead of the thinking that was supporting the parallel, but unarguably more complicated, inclusion agenda in schools (see Farrell and Ainscow 2003; Mittler 2003; Thomas and Loxley 2001). The Tomlinson Report was followed by a two-year period of intensive national dissemination, the impact of which was then extensively reported by the Learning and Skills Development Agency (LSDA) (Further Education Development Agency (FEDA) 1988). (LSDA was formerly FEDA and evolved in 2006 into two organizations – the Learning and Skills Network and the Quality Improvement Agency.) Tomlinson's principle of shifting funding away from specialist courses to a system which supported individuals on courses of their choice resulted in improved mainstream inclusion for students with sensory and physical impairments and specific learning difficulties. It did much to influence colleges' attitudes and understanding and ultimately encouraged the shift from segregative cultures to more inclusive cultures (FEDA 1998; LSDA 2003).

Ofsted's interpretation of inclusive education

The change in inspection regimes from the Further Education Funding Council (FEFC) to Ofsted (DfES 1999) could have been a challenge, potentially, to continued progress in the development of inclusive education in FE. Ofsted's concern with standards and performance, measured against governmentally prescribed national targets for attainment, could have been in conflict with the successful inclusion of those learners who may not easily achieve at Level 2 or, indeed, Level 3. This kind of achievement may also be irrelevant or unhelpful to such students in moving on in life and employment. So it is encouraging that Ofsted has recently committed to including a judgement in its inspection of colleges about 'the extent to which a college is educationally and socially inclusive' (Ofsted 2005), although this occurred some nine years after Tomlinson. This could move the development of inclusive education forward positively and quickly by providing models of good practice and public access to national information about how inclusive further education may be achieved. Although Ofsted offers a somewhat underdeveloped definition of inclusive education which emphasizes social inclusion and ducks the issue of how educational inclusion may be more broadly understood, it does capture the underpinning ideologies of meeting human rights and taking collective responsibility for all learners. Ofsted defines inclusion as 'the efforts made to increase access to education and training for all members of the community especially those who might not otherwise attend college' (Ofsted 2005). There is an implicit expectation in this that all colleges should strive to create inclusive cultures in which 'each learner matters' (Ofsted 2005, p. 85) and to create learning communities in which the values of tolerance and respect are much in evidence.

In its publication 'Why Colleges Succeed' (Ofsted 2005), Ofsted provides examples of colleges which have had 'an exemplary response to educational and social inclusion'. For one college this response is described as 'commitment to equality of opportunity and equity, which is not merely the-oretical ... *but* ... devotes considerable energy to practical activity and staff training which ensures that it is an inclusive community, valuing each individual's contribution and cele-brating diversity'. Another college's ethos is described as 'fos-tering a strong social, academic and spiritual atmosphere, enabling all students to work together with a shared sense of purpose and mutual respect' (Ofsted 2004). Although, perhaps unusually for Ofsted, these are not deconstructed as measurable performance indicators (at least not yet), the message is transparent.

The CSIE's 'Index for Inclusion'

The CSIE's 'Index for Inclusion', which is recommended by DfES (DfES 2001) and now widely used by schools, also has much to offer FE. It goes further than Ofsted in that it *does* provide indicators and deconstructs effective inclusion in terms of how well institutional cultures, policies and practices identify the barriers to learning and participation, decide on their own priorities for change and evaluate their progress. The indicators and linked questions for each of the dimensions of culture, practice and policy are written in easily understood language; for example, 'Do staff learn how to counter bullying, including racism, sexism and homophobia?' (CSIE 2001, p. 4).

For the CSIE, inclusion involves:

- valuing all students and staff equally
- increasing the participation of students in, and reducing their exclusion from, the cultures, curricula and communities of local schools
- restructuring the cultures, policies and practices (in schools) so that they respond to the diversity of students in the locality
- reducing barriers to learning and participation for all students, not only those with impairments or those who are categorized as 'having special educational needs'
- learning from attempts to overcome barriers to the access and participation of particular students to make changes for the benefit of students more widely
- viewing the differences between students as a resource to support learning, rather than as problems to be overcome
- acknowledging the right of students to an education in their locality
- improving schools for staff as well as for students
- emphasizing the role of schools in building community and developing values, as well as in increasing achievement
- fostering mutually sustaining relationships between schools and communities
- recognizing that inclusion in education is one aspect of inclusion in society.

The challenge for colleges

Inclusive education challenges colleges as never before to create institutional cultures, systems, policies and practices that are inherently inclusive. In meeting the requirements of the law through SENDA and in proactively embedding these into colleges' mission and strategic planning, colleges are already becoming more inclusive. But it is not enough that learners of all abilities, backgrounds and aspirations are provided for. Inclusive education requires colleges to go further to ensure that all learners are welcomed, encouraged, valued and treated with respect, and that expectations for all learners are high and that everyone reaches his or her potential. Both the new Ofsted *Handbook for Inspecting Colleges* and the CSIE's 'Index for Inclusion' provide long lists of success factors, which should exercise even the most committed colleges for some time to come.

Creating inclusive classrooms

Whilst it is undoubtedly true that teachers will find it easier to create inclusive classrooms in colleges which are working towards developing inclusive cultures, policies and practices, there are steps that lecturers can take within their own classrooms to create more inclusive learning environments.

The traditional pulse of further education already drives inclusive education and is gathering momentum through new laws in this country. It is also being driven forward by the immediate and acute awareness in all civilized societies across the world of the need to combat intolerance and hatred on the grounds of racial, religious and cultural differences. Inclusive education can happen naturally in every classroom if the lecturer has the 'right' mindset about the differences learners present. This 'right' mindset comes from an innate belief that every learner can succeed, that every learner is worth the effort, and that every learner has equal value. From this 'right' thinking, combined with confidence and some skills to teach classes in which learners may lack confidence, maturity, self-belief, skills, knowledge or understanding, inclusive learning environments will emerge.

This book will equip you with many of the teaching skills you will need to manage diversity and to improve the experience of every one of your learners. The value system and the framework for 'inclusive thinking' which is required for these skills to have a purpose and be put to good use is likely to be already within you. Inclusive education '... demands a fundamental conviction that all human beings are of absolutely equal worth simply by virtue of being human' (Rustemeir 2002).

2 English for Speakers of Other Languages

Working within the context of inclusive education described in Chapter 1, this chapter will focus on supporting the English for Speakers of Other Languages (ESOL) learners in your classroom. Up to one million people in England do not speak English as their first language 'Skills for Life, Focus on delivery (DfES 2003) and many of these may be the learners you are likely to encounter in further education.

ESOL students in the UK might bring a wide range of skills, abilities and experience from varying cultures and backgrounds as well as diverse languages to your classroom. They might include individuals who are highly qualified in their own countries of origin as well as others who have literacy or language needs in their first language. In addition to the demands presented by particular subject specialist and/or vocational areas, many ESOL learners may also face challenges in acquiring English language skills and accessing the dominant culture in the UK.

Defining the terms

Some ESOL students may be newly arrived asylum seekers, in the process of applying for indefinite leave to remain (commonly known as 'ILR') or they may be refugees with more secure rights (please see Chapter 3). Others may be long settled in the UK and well-established residents, with spouses and work permits. There may even be some second generation immigrants and younger people. The different terms used are sometimes very confusing and emotively charged, especially in debates in the media, so within the context of inclusive education, it might be more helpful to disregard the definitions surrounding students' residential status and to focus on their needs as speakers of other languages.

There is similar confusion surrounding the terms used to describe English language teaching, such as ESL – English as a Second Language; EAL – English as an Additional Language; ESP – English for Special/Specific Purposes; and EAP – English for Academic Purposes, but the term currently favoured in UK post-compulsory education is ESOL.

In addition, many people are uncertain about the difference between (T)ESOL and (T)EFL – (Teaching) English as a Foreign Language. While both involve the teaching of English language, the latter tends to refer to a different target group of learners, namely, those who have chosen to learn English for pleasure, work or education, for example, au pairs living and working in the UK for a year before returning to their own countries, or business people who recognize English as an international language and wish to apply it in their commerce. (T)ESOL refers to those learners who speak a different mother tongue but who intend to take up permanent residence within the UK (Target 2003).

Traditionally, teaching EFL either within the UK or abroad has been an important and lucrative market, largely in the private sector which focuses on the overseas visitor who is likely to be affluent, formally educated in their country of origin and often, but not necessarily, European. In EFL teaching, attention is mainly directed towards grammatical structures, reading and writing skills. Teaching ESOL, however, is based in the UK within the state and the private sectors and it focuses on the language needed for settling into a new culture initially, but not exclusively, through the communicative skills of speaking and listening, enabling learners to participate in the political, social and economic life of the country. While there are significant differences between EFL and ESOL, both involve teaching English language so that it is possible for teachers to move between the two. Recent initiatives, such as the development of the Adult Core Curriculum, are closing the gap between EFL and ESOL, although the different kinds of learners in EFL and ESOL remain distinct.

Who are these ESOL learners?

Britain's multicultural heritage provides evidence of descendants from central and eastern Europe in the shape of the Romans, Normans and their Breton and Flemish allies, as well as the first Africans who came as soldiers of the Roman army. Later, other groups, such as the French Huguenots and Russian Jews, fled religious pogroms to settle in this country. As a result of the two world wars, refugees from Belgium, Spanish Basques, more Jewish settlers, Poles and Hungarians sought sanctuary here. At different times in the twentieth century, world refugees from Uganda, Chile, Vietnam, Bosnia, Somalia, Eritrea, Afghanistan, Iraq, Zimbabwe and many other countries have also made their homes in the UK. In a survey conducted by the Refugee Council (Knox 1997), it was found that the majority of refugees were highly qualified and successful in their home countries, often coming from professional backgrounds with skills exceeding the levels of the general British population.

For centuries, then, people from all over the world have come to settle in the UK for a variety of reasons; some seek a better life and more challenging opportunities, others fear persecution and are driven to escape danger and civil war in their own countries. The history of immigration provides a rich source of diversity and today's ESOL learners are no exception. Throughout Britain there are communities of people whose first languages may range from Amaric, Bengali, Chinese, Farsi, Somali and Turkish to Urdu. Those with very limited English language skills are likely to be placed within discrete English language classes in the learning and skills sector, while others with more advanced English language skills may well be engaged in studying a variety of subjects or vocational areas alongside native speakers of English in both higher and further education.

Theories of bilingualism and second language acquisition

Many ESOL learners may be multilingual, but described as bilingual; even though the term 'bilingual' strictly refers to fluency in only two languages, it is sometimes applied to indicate an ability to use more than two languages.

Early, naive theories of second language acquisition tended to make comparisons with learning a first language or mother tongue. Such theories also suggested that there were only certain levels of learning and knowing of any two languages that could be attained simultaneously; for example, that there was only a certain amount of space in the brain to cope with the acquisition of one language at a time! These theories have sometimes been presented diagramatically as a set of scales, with a second language increasing at the expense of the first language or in a sketch of two language balloons, showing the mono-lingual person with one well-filled balloon in his or her head, while the bilingual has two half-filled balloons (Baker 2002).

Subconsciously, these ideas have been absorbed and repeated by many people and are often part of a 'commonsense' understanding of what it means to be bilingual: namely, to have two languages operating separately in a restricted space, although research has shown it is wrong to make these assumptions (Baker 2002). Such ideas have sometimes encouraged a notion of first language interference that has negative implications for acquiring additional languages. In challenging this notion, Jyoti Nayar (2004) describes how children learn a first language easily and naturally so that 'by the age of three we children used three languages separately and without mixing', in what Swain (1972) calls 'multilingualism as the first language'.

Later research of second language acquisition has investigated theories of first language acquisition and the sequences or patterns of how this development takes place and showed that 'the further the child moves towards a balanced bilingualism, the greater the likelihood of cognitive advantages' (Baker 2002). In other words, at the first level of learning when (both) languages are inadequately developed there may be negative cognitive effects but as language proficiency advances in at least one of the languages, the cognitive effects will be balanced until greater competence is achieved in two or more languages. Therefore, there are positive advantages for the cognitive development of bi/multilinguals over monolinguals. The implications of this 'Thresholds Theory' are relevant to teachers and they have been expressed by Cummins (Baker 2002) in terms of basic interpersonal communicative skills (BICS) and cognitive/academic language proficiency (CALP).

BICS refers to the everyday language of survival that is 'context embedded', in which ESOL learners may function at a basic level of communication, drawing upon face-to-face cues, and verbal and non-verbal support in everyday situations. It is claimed that this may take up to two years to acquire (Baker 2002). In contrast, CALP, which may only be achieved after five to eight years or more, is 'context reduced' and is specific to academic situations which require individuals to apply higher thinking skills, such as analysis, synthesis and evaluation (Baker 2002). Very often in the learning and skills sector, those ESOL learners who have transferred from discreet ESOL classes to mainstream vocational courses might well have achieved BICS but not yet CALP. They are likely to appear ready to be taught in the second or other language but they may find it much more challenging to understand the content of the curriculum and/or to engage in the higher order cognitive processes of the classroom, such as synthesis, discussion, analysis and evaluation. Strategies for responding to this are suggested at the end of the chapter.

These theories of second language acquisition have been further supplemented by behaviourist explanations in the 1940s and 1950s, the innatism of Chomsky's Universal Grammar and interactionists such as Piaget and Vygotsky. If you would like to explore any of these in more detail, references are provided at the end of this book.

National context

In response to Sir Claus Moser's landmark report *A Fresh Start* (DfEE 1999a), in which it was claimed that up to seven million

Table 1 The national standards for adult literacy with examples and school equivalents (DfES 2003, p. 36).

National Standard	Adults are able to	National Curriculum level
Entry 1	Read and obtain information from common signs and symbols.	Level 1 (age 5)
Entry 2	Use punctuation correctly, including capital letters, full stops and question marks.	Level 2 (age 7)
Entry 3	Organize writing in short paragraphs.	Level 3 (age 9)
Level 1	Identify the main points and specific details in texts.	Level 4 (age 11)
Level 2	Read and understand a range of texts of varying complexity accurately and independently.	GCSE A*–C (age 16)

adults in England could not read or write at the level expected of an 11-year-old, the Government launched its Skills for Life initiative in 2001 – a national strategy for improving the standards of adult language, literacy and numeracy skills. This involved setting ambitious targets that were linked to the funding and development of Adult Core Curricula in ESOL, Literacy and Numeracy. The introduction of the Adult ESOL Core Curriculum in 2002 clearly lays out levels of achievement, starting from Entry 1, 2 and 3 to Levels 1 and 2, which correspond to the National Curriculum levels for schools (see Table 1).

These curriculum levels indicate what ESOL learners should be able to demonstrate in the different skills at each level and may provide helpful guidance for teachers about what to expect from their learners and also how to support their needs on different programmes as well as applying appropriate criteria when interviewing and selecting individuals for particular courses.

Language skills and spiky profiles

For purposes of convenience, teachers of ESOL classify the acquisition of knowledge of English language in terms of four skills, namely, speaking, listening, reading and writing, although in reality these overlap and are not so simply separated. It is not uncommon for ESOL learners to demonstrate varying levels of achievement in each of these skills simultaneously. For example, an individual ESOL learner may be highly competent in reading and writing with less developed skills in speaking and listening or, alternatively, confident and articulate in speaking and listening, but lacking skills in reading and writing. These uneven language skills are sometimes referred to as 'spiky profiles' and indicate those particular skills that would need urgent attention and support if individuals are to progress and achieve in their specific subject–specialist areas.

Spiky profiles may be attributed to the role of the first language in the acquisition of an additional language or other factors related to self-esteem, confidence, previous experience and/or formal education. In gaining these skills, ESOL learners may demonstrate fluency over accuracy or vice versa, and it will be the specific demands of the subject specialism that are likely to determine the priorities given to error correction in this respect. For example, for a clinician or pharmacist, being unable to distinguish the difference in speech between '50' and '15' might have life-threatening repercussions, while for a computer operator, it might cause minor inconvenience. Similarly, having competent writing skills may be more important in some occupations, such as journalism, rather than others, such as bus driving. Decisions about what to correct in terms of accuracy or fluency will depend on the requirements of the subject specialism and intended vocational or professional directions.

Valuing multilingualism, belonging and identity

Whatever seems most relevant to your situation, it is important for teachers to value multilingualism as an asset to learning and cognitive development and to recognize the complexity of the process involved in acquiring an additional language with its implications for motivation, self-esteem and identity, as well as for personal development and growth in confidence. Language is inextricably linked with personal history and individual identity. Annette Zera's opening address to the annual conference of the National Association for Teaching English and Community Languages to Adults (NATECLA) in July 2004 reminded ESOL practitioners and delegates of the connections between citizenship, identity and belonging and posed the question about how easy (or not) it is for ESOL learners to feel a sense of belonging within the classroom.

Identity is about who we are as individuals, our distinctiveness, our very selves; about how securely we face the world and how confidently we manage and express ourselves (Zera 2004). Through language, we recognize a sense of belonging to a particular group of people joined together by any number of factors such as geography, race, ethnicity, gender, religion and language. It must be the ultimate achievement of the inclusion agenda to secure that sense of belonging for each learner within the classroom. And for ESOL learners this may present particular challenges for teachers who need to take into account unfamiliar aspects of their cultural identities, languages, previous education and experiences.

Strategies and practices to embed diversity and inclusion

Although there are a list of practical suggestions at the end of this section, it should be stressed that there are no simple 'quick fixes' or shortcuts to getting to know your individual learners and their needs, or to encourage in them a sense of belonging and identity. For those feeling inexperienced, untrained or unsupported in working with ESOL learners, it may be helpful to recommend some starting points, bearing in mind that each learner is unique and what works for one may not for another. While it is inevitably a time-consuming process of ongoing discovery and learning that doesn't always have a finite destination, there are some basic guidelines for supporting ESOL learners, many of which would constitute good practice for all learners.

It is perhaps worth noting the mismatch in power relations between any teacher and his or her learners and the way in which this may be accentuated by the ability of those who control the classroom discourse through language, simultaneously acting as gatekeepers to the social goods and services of the dominant community (Mitchell and Myles 1998). All learners are subject to this but ESOL learners may be even more susceptible, so that to establish an inclusive environment based on social justice and equality within the classroom will present challenges.

Furthermore, implicit assumptions about bilingualism referred to earlier may need to be recognized and addressed. These may be expressed in a number of ways, such as making negative judgements about an ESOL learner's intellectual ability based upon his or her inability to express him or herself in English, leading to low expectations and/or even to misinterpretation as a deeper-seated learning difficulty (Gillborn and Gipps 1996, cited in Smyth 2003). Such implicit assumptions may also lead to inappropriate use of simplified, pidgin English and/or speaking very loudly in a patronizing fashion, or making the assumption that bilingual students need to deny their own origins and culture and become monolingual in order to succeed (Smyth 2003). At best, while these responses may be described as well intentioned, they illustrate a deficit view of bilingualism which is negatively defined by its failure to conform to the white, middle-class, monolinguistic 'norm' of the dominant UK culture.

Beyond these wider issues of social context, it is important to find out what you can about your individual ESOL learners. Information about a student may provide insights into the kind of support that would be appropriate. This information includes the name by which he or she prefers to be called and how that is pronounced, his or her first language and other languages and competence in each, previous formal education (or not), arrival in the UK, details of family, friends or relatives and future intentions and aspirations. Some of this information may be readily accessible, but the ESOL learner may be reluctant to disclose other aspects and so his or her reasons should be respected and treated with sensitivity. It may be helpful in establishing a positive relationship to learn how to say 'hello' or 'thank you' in his or her language and/or to display some of this language in the classroom, personally valuing his or her identity and cultural origins.

Another way of valuing ESOL learners is to draw on their knowledge and experience of other languages and cultures and to create opportunities for them to share and demonstrate this within the context of the subject specialism, thereby enhancing the multicultural and multilinguistic nature of the class without falling into the trap of tokenism. The way in which small group activities are set up should enable ESOL learners to demonstrate what they know and can do rather than exposing their weaknesses in English language. For example, in conducting small group work, the ESOL learner may be practically adept but not confident in reporting back or writing up on flipchart paper what has been observed, so these tasks could be shared out, encouraging sharing and collaboration among group members.

Furthermore, in planning curriculum activities it would be useful to analyse the language needed in terms of the functions, structures and specialist vocabulary so that potential problems may be pre-empted before they occur. The way in which this might be done is illustrated in Table 2.

In those institutions where ESOL specialists and resources are available, it might be helpful to consult language specialists and to enlist their assistance in analysing the language of your subject-specialist area in more detail to raise awareness of how this can be presented and practised and to consider how it is embedded (and often taken for granted) within the subject specialism. Furthermore, it might be helpful to liaise closely with language support workers so that their work with individual ESOL learners either within or outside the classroom relates to the requirements and needs of your own subject-specialist area.

The distinction between BICS and CALP is also worth noting. It is important for teachers to acknowledge that ESOL learners' linguistic knowledge and understanding may be highly developed, even though they are not in a position at a particular

Table 2 Language analysis of functions, structure and vocabulary in different subject areas

Curriculum activity or subject specialism	Function/s	Structure/ examples of language	Specialist vocabulary
Scientific experiment	Observing, identifying, comparing, hypothesizing, predicting, reporting	Passive structures, e.g. water is placed in a beaker; conditionals, e.g. if the heat is reduced, then the water stops boiling, etc.	Beaker, Bunsen burner; pipette, etc.
Leisure/tourism	Advertising, persuasive language	Language of brochures and use of adjectives, e.g. glorious, sun-drenched beaches; quaint, cobbled streets, etc.	Bed and breakfast; double room; twin room; self-catering, etc.

point in time to produce language which is beyond the level of BICS. If they are to achieve CALP, it is essential that they are exposed to new language structures and that teachers and others in the class model and provide opportunities for them to put these language skills into practice. Use of context, non-verbal cues, visual aids and demonstration might all be used to aid the transition from BICS to CALP.

Furthermore, use of ESOL learners' own languages, particularly if these are shared with another member of the class, might be applied in certain situations and might prove an asset in securing the learning of a difficult concept as well as the English language. Many teachers who don't share the ESOL learners' first language may feel a little uncomfortable and insecure in not being able to control a dialogue in which they are unable to participate, but it might be helpful if they see it as putting themselves in a similar position to the ESOL learner of not always being in control linguistically. This is about creating a space for individual learning and the development of trust which serves to value their identity, build confidence and self-esteem and brings us back to the original point of this exercise in differentiation and inclusion – namely, a sense of belonging within the classroom.

Good luck!

Practical suggestions

Some more practical suggestions for supporting ESOL learners are given below, many of which would constitute good practice for all learners.

Use plain English, for example:

- Avoid idioms, figurative language and colloquialisms, for example, 'chalk and cheese', 'turning your nose up' or 'raining cats and dogs'. Be aware of similar sounding words, such as fringe and fridge, cheap and chic, and thirty and thirteen.
- Avoid digressions and anecdotes – students may find it hard to distinguish them from the actual subject matter.
- Use consistent intonation patterns, especially when giving instructions, for example, stress the same key words each time you repeat them.
- Explain technical and subject language and check understanding. Confusion can arise when words have an everyday meaning and a different technical meaning, such as 'mouse' in computing.
- Use short sentences.

Repeat key vocabulary and concepts and summarize:

- At the beginning of each lesson or activity, define the purpose of the lesson and say what you are going to do in relation to the last session.
- Work out beforehand the key concepts you want students to learn and remember. Repeat them frequently as a lesson progresses.
- Summarize frequently as this gives students a second chance to pick up key information.

- When talking, be explicit about the information you are giving; for example, 'my first point is' ... 'now I am going to move on to my second point', 'it is essential to note that...'.
- Write key words on the whiteboard or OHT.
- Organize staged lessons – tell students very clearly when you are moving from one stage of a lesson to another and reinforce this with written instructions on the whiteboard.

3 Refugee students in the FE classroom

Who is a refugee? Confusion surrounding terminology

'As is often the case, Further Education (FE) is the sector in which least provision is made, and it is argued by many that as a way of maximising benefits to both individual students and the community, this is the sector that needs the most thorough review.' (Freeman 1977)

The above is a statement taken from research conducted almost 30 years ago. However, it could be argued that little has changed since then and the conclusions reached are even more applicable today.

'Refugee', 'asylum seeker', 'indefinite leave to remain': these are all terms that are used, often interchangeably, but how many of us are really aware of what they actually mean? Yet, if individual staff can't get the terminology right, then how can the support students receive in the classroom be effectively targeted? What does support and terminology have in common, you might ask? Well, they can help in the explanation of why a student is in your classroom one day and absent from it the next.

On 22 June 2005, the much-awaited Asylum and Nationality Bill was brought before the UK Parliament. The bill promises to implement most of the measures mentioned in the Government's five-year plan on asylum and immigration, entitled 'Controlling our borders: Making migration work for Britain' (see www.brc.uk.org for the document in full).

Although the Bill is primarily designed to look at controlled migration and nationality, there are issues concerning those with indefinite leave to remain.

Refugee status

In the UK, a person is recognized as a refugee once their application for asylum has been accepted by the Home Office. Decisions on who is granted refugee status are made by the Integrated Casework Unit of the Home Office. Claims are assessed according to the current political situation in a country of origin and evidence of a country's human rights record. Additionally, claims are increasingly assessed against medical evidence of abuse and torture, perhaps most importantly for those involved in the teaching profession. It is up to the individual to prove that they meet the criteria laid down by the 1951 Geneva Convention relating to the status of refugees (see www.brc.org).

Indefinite leave to remain

Since August 2005, refugees are no longer entitled to indefinite leave to remain (ILR) – all refugees are granted an initial stay of five years. Once the five years are over, the case is subject to review and factors such as the current political situation in the country of origin are looked at by the Home Office. Home Office assessors decide whether that individual is no longer in fear of persecution. Technically, at that stage, refugees could be faced with the harrowing prospect of forced removal from the UK. If not, they should be given ILR. Recently, there has been debate about the additional tests surrounding competence in English being linked to leave to remain. If the initial application is refused, the individual has the right to appeal to the Immigration Appeals Tribunal.

Asylum seeker

An asylum seeker is best described as an individual who has crossed a border in order to seek safety. In the UK context, an asylum seeker is someone who is awaiting a decision from the Home Office as to whether they can remain in the country or not.

Table 3 Language spoken in countries of origin

Country of origin	Main (and secondary) language/s spoken
Iran	Farsi (Azerbaijani)
China	Mandarin (Cantonese)
Iraq	Arabic (Kurdish)
Somalia	Somali (Arabic)
Zimbabwe	English (Shona)
Democratic Republic of Congo	French (Lingala)
Eritrea	Tigrinya (Tigre)
Sudan	Arabic (Dinka)
Pakistan	Urdu (Punjabi)

Countries of origin and languages spoken

Various parts of the world suffered conflict and upheaval in 2004. This was reflected in the countries of origin of those seeking asylum in the UK (Home Office 2004). This is illustrated in Table 3. Also shown in the table are the main languages spoken in the country together with the second main language spoken (Katzner 1995).

Traumatic events – some background information

Migration is in itself an upheaval: both challenging and stressful. When the process involves traumatic events, the stress involved commonly surpasses an individual's or family's natural coping mechanisms (Senior 2002).

It is important to remember that refugee students encompass myriad of backgrounds and, as such, encounter varying degrees of trauma, stress and other complex experiences. What is clear, however, is that despite their backgrounds, all students encounter some kind of guilt. Guilt at being unable to help other family members also experiencing difficulties, guilt at being the 'fortunate' ones who escaped, and guilt at being powerless.

In the classroom, teachers need to remember that:

- Students come with a variety of educational experiences.
- Some students may have had no formal education at all.
- Some students might have witnessed or been party to brutal acts.
- As a result of prior experiences, students may be suffering post-traumatic stress disorder (PTSD) or other medical conditions which make it difficult to concentrate.
- Some students may need to engage in family, legal or religious matters connected with their immigration status which may mean absences from class (see below).
- A change in status might have occurred – previously middle-class families may find themselves having to wait for others to provide support to them.
- A reversal in roles might have occurred – in their previous home, the father might have been the main breadwinner, only to find here that this is no longer the case.

Understanding coping mechanisms within the contest of learning. How might students react?

Bolloten and Spafford (1998) state that some teachers may sometimes show a reluctance to engage with the experiences of refugee students. They argue that their main fear is being overwhelmed by the complexity of the situation, the needs refugee students may have and their anxieties. All these, they state, may cause some teachers to become withdrawn or to distance themselves from these students.

Alternatively, some teachers do not know where their competence ends. With the very best of intentions, they may find themselves becoming more and more involved in the students' lives and consequently become the first port of call for that student. Teaching therefore not only encompasses that which takes place in the classroom, but also extends to advice on housing needs, medical issues and documentation regarding legal status. Here the anecdotal evidence becomes apparent – the teachers of refugee students are not only teachers, but social workers, housing advisers and legal advisers without training.

Again, it is important to remember that all students are individual and as such no two experiences can be regarded as the same, nor should they be. The following, however, are some of the behaviours refugee students in post-compulsory settings might exhibit.

- Long periods of silence in the classroom – despite a number of strategies utilized by teachers – may lead teachers and others to start labelling students as having 'mental health' needs.
- A desire to constantly please the teacher – and often hiding their true feelings. This could mean refugee students agreeing with the teacher at every opportunity and having a permanent smile on their face. Their aim is to be seen as a model student. Despite reassurances, some refugee students still perceive there to be a link between the educational setting they find themselves in and the Home Office and subsequently feel that if they behave in an ideal way, they are more likely to be allowed to remain in the country.
- Students may find it difficult to engage in group work or role-play because of the difficulties encountered in forming relationships after previous negative experiences. Also, students could find it difficult to separate reality from fiction when working with case studies, for example.
- Students may become sad at times and suffer from uncontrollable outbursts of tears. This can occur as a reaction to something minor said within the classroom. Often the trigger is something out of the teacher's control and takes place outside the classroom.
- The complete opposite may occur. Outbursts of rage, though quite rare, have been reported. These can result from the frustration of not being able to resort to language to explain points of view, etc.
- An attachment to the teacher. Often, the teacher is one of the few permanent people in the refugee students' lives.

The student may take to following the teacher around. Also, inappropriate questions might be asked, for example, wanting to know more and more about the teacher. This is especially the case with younger refugee students who, as unaccompanied minors, find the need to bond with an adult in a position of authority.

- Lateness and absence due to their status. Students can be re-housed overnight. Power, Whitty and Youdell (1998) look at how some refugee students continued to travel from their new accommodation to their 'old' educational settings, often for several hours at a time.

- Some students may be here one day and find themselves in another area altogether the next and attending classes at the institution near the former location becomes impossible. Rutter and Jones (1998) argue that the lack of information given to refugee students means that they are faced with uncertainty and limited continuity which both contribute to the obstacles they face.

Ensuring flexibility in the learning environment

Teachers in general are being faced with increasingly overwhelming burdens. Ofsted and the Adult Learning Inspectorate (ALI) require teachers to keep and continuously monitor detailed records, whether they be teaching plans or individual records on students. Senior management teams in educational institutions are under increasing pressure to be seen to monitor the quality of the teaching and learning within their establishments. The introduction of the Adult Core Curriculum has, some would say, encouraged teachers to become more fixed in their teaching and less likely to be innovative and fluid.

As teachers, we are all being encouraged to retain information that promotes the view that learning is lifelong. Very rare is the teacher who doesn't have a portfolio of some sort or other that contains evidence of targets met and milestones reached during their teaching careers. Increasingly, these portfolios have become burdensome, as teachers struggle ever harder to meet the demands of an 'audit culture' in FE.

What is the role of the teacher in all of this?

What all of this indicates is that teachers are increasingly less likely to be fluid, organic and responsive to situations as they arise in the classroom. The following are some suggestions for teachers to look at when trying to meet the needs of refugee students.

- The need to create a 'psychologically safe' environment for 'success' to take place – it is important to note here that we are not only concerned with measurable achievement. Success could be seen as something as basic as attendance at classes, depending on the starting point of the student.
- The 'good practice' suggestion to allow students to have an input into the lesson – ownership needs to be extended and seen to belong to both the student and the teacher – real partnerships can be formed at this time, which can be the base for future learning.
- The need to ensure that lessons are 'fluid and organic', as opposed to hard and stringent rules being in place. Picture the scenario: a teacher could come with a meticulously planned lesson, but events reported in the media over-night or on the same day could encourage students to want to talk about other matters. A resourceful teacher should incorporate this new information within that lesson and not remain steadfast to the original plan.
- The need to allow students to talk sometimes; not only for 'practice' purposes but to allow the class to take on an almost 'cathartic' process. Students who have remained 'silent' for many lessons might suddenly start relaying harrowing experiences which could be the starting point for them moving on to the next phase of their lives. This is particularly concerning for some teachers, as they might feel that matters are being taken out of their control. However, what almost always occurs is that the student, together with the other class members, will come to a natural decision as to when to stop, allowing the class to move on.

Providing support to teachers working under 'intense' conditions

Working with refugee students, as is the case with all students, can be an exciting, engaging and unique experience. However, it can also be demanding, both in terms of time and emotional requirements. As previously stated, teachers are being increasingly asked to keep and maintain detailed records. This paperwork, together with the emotional requirements that are created and the sense of helplessness in being unable to meet the needs of the student, can at times be overwhelming for the teacher. The difficulties faced by the teacher often become apparent when it is too late and the teacher has suffered. In order for students to be supported appropriately, we must not forget the needs of the teacher providing that support. It is often this part of the relationship that is overlooked. The following are some areas for managers to look at concerning how best to support teachers with refugee students in their classes.

- Teachers need to have a 'buddy' within the same or another department. An individual is needed who can act as a 'sounding board' for that teacher, whether for discussion regarding teaching methods or purely to provide an opportunity to move away from the support environment.
- Access is needed to high-quality training regarding the psychological needs of refugee students, such as that provided by the British Refugee Council. It is important to remember that, first and foremost, the individual is a teacher and should not be expected to take on more than they are able, experienced or qualified to do.
- Teachers need to develop their listening skills, particularly 'active' listening skills. It is important that this is taught, together with non-verbal communication – being able to pick up on the cues within the classroom is invaluable.
- Teachers need to be aware of outside agencies and the support they provide. Teachers need to know when their expertise ends and when to refer the situation on.
- Teachers can form links with members of local community groups. These are invaluable when seeking information on

particular matters or when referring on students in your class. This is particularly important when a student is isolated.

Conclusions

Working with refugee students as described is clearly an experience like no other. The advantages that exposure to different ways of living, different educational systems and different languages bring are unique. In order for all to benefit from this exposure, however, systems and strategies need to be in place.

The euphoria created when a refugee student reaches a goal, no matter how small or great, is indescribable. The most successful educational institutions are those that foresee the issues and plan effectively. Although the planning can in no way be expected to take care of everything, what it can do is ensure that the basics are covered, leaving time and other resources to be devoted to other matters as and when they arise.

4 What's in a name?
Teaching support staff

They are known by a number of different names: language support teachers; additional support workers; learning support workers and curriculum support workers. The departments they are employed in similarly have a variety of names – language support departments, additional support departments and learning support departments, to name but a few.

Although the name might change, together with fashions surrounding the name in use at any one time, what doesn't change is the support these individuals can provide. This can make the difference between students receiving high-quality input, leading to an overall cohesive educational experience, or students benefiting from an additional adult in the room providing support that is not valued and consequently that individual losing morale in the process.

Although these departments may employ staff in assistant capacities and roles (for further discussion see Fox (2001) and Farrell (2000)), it is the issues affecting qualified support teachers in post-compulsory settings that will form the basis of the discussion that will take place in this chapter.

Managing overall support – some strategies for good practice

For any department to work well, there is a need to analyse and review practices regularly. An ideal way of carrying this out is to periodically conduct an audit of existing practices. Basic as it may appear, only by looking at what is being carried out can what is to be improved be seen. For anyone intending to conduct an audit, some of the areas that need to be looked at are:

- The departmental policy – does it exist? This could be regarded as forming the bedrock of any department. What is the policy on the deployment of staff? Has support taken place on a needs basis or purely on historical links with departments being formed and remaining in place? Even less secure, and much less justifiable, has deployment existed solely as a result of friendships between managers?

- Are support roles and responsibilities clearly identified and relayed to those concerned? An effective manager needs to ensure that both the support teacher and the mainstream teacher are clear on the professional relationship that needs to exist and what they can expect from each other. Although initially time-consuming, in the long run this will be effective because misunderstandings are less likely to occur. Therefore, less time will be dedicated to solving misunderstandings.

- Is an induction programme available in which new members of the department are given an overall intro-duction to the aims and goals of the department? If an induction programme exists, how often is it updated? Ideally, updating should occur frequently and take into account the opinions of newer members of staff. This will ensure that the programme remains informative and relevant.

- Does a mentoring or 'buddy' system exist? New and existing members of staff need to have a means of gaining support for themselves. It is important not to under-estimate the need for an avenue for support teachers to air their views and opinions or somewhere to seek advice other than within the department sometimes, if appropriate.

- Are support teachers encouraged to engage in planning and liaison time with their 'host' teachers? This is invaluable with regards to the self-esteem of the support teacher.

- Are job descriptions given to all members of staff, regardless of the hours they work? This provides clarity and ensures individuals concerned remain focused and engaged.

- Do support teachers play an active part in assessment? There is a tendency for individual teachers to carry out their work in isolation. However, post-compulsory education is increasingly demanding informal and formal assessment (Armitage and Bryant 2001). If assessment of the student is carried out by both teachers, then a more rounded picture of whether success has been achieved can be obtained.
- Resources are an area often overlooked. These can be as basic as access to storage space or having a desk to prepare work on. If individual desks are considered impossible, are there means to provide shared space?

Ensuring clarity in roles and expectations

In order for support to be effective and to avoid conflict and the breakdown of professional relationships, there is a need to ensure clarity exists in the roles of both the support teacher and the mainstream teacher and to specify what each one can realistically expect or should expect from the other. Clear parameters need to be set and revisited often. Any discussion or documentation resulting should take into account some of the following:

- There needs to be clear discussion and acceptance of the type of support that is to be provided. Often support, as previously mentioned, could have occurred on an historical basis, the argument being that a particular department has always received support. Alternatively, a 'bidding' process could have been in operation – this is where individual departments have 'bid' for support and this has then supposedly occurred on a needs basis. Similarly, in the classroom, the support teacher might have become used to providing targeted support to one or two students. Here, the teacher sees their role as being limited to working with two or three students. Other support models might include input occurring at the planning stage resulting in more of a teaching partnership. In best practice, roles can be reversed and the support teacher might on occasions lead the session, with the mainstream teacher providing the support (for further discussion of this model of teaching see Bourne and McPake (1991)).

- Planning and liaison time needs to be in existence and is one of the core principles of effective support teaching. This is important in order to recognize the skills, experience and expertise of the support teacher and not to have any area overlooked. If this is not addressed, there is a tendency for the support teacher to be seen as a 'guest' and not really having any ownership of the lesson. This is also important from the view of the students – they will have a tendency to see the mainstream teacher as the only fully qualified individual and subsequently the support teacher's role may be undermined.

- An up-to-date job description is needed for all staff, regardless of whether they are full time, fractional or hourly paid. This is needed to ensure all concerned are familiar with the expectations of the role. This measure should eliminate situations in which highly qualified teachers are used as little more than photocopying assistants – anecdotal evidence informs us that this has sometimes occurred in FE institutions not providing full guidance on job descriptions.

- A good balance of in-class support and administrative roles. It is important not to underestimate the records and documentation that are required to be kept. In order for that to take place, time to carry out the administration needs to be built into the timetable.

- Individual meetings with the line manager are needed at regular intervals in order that any issues can be resolved early and before they escalate and affect the support provided. This also provides a forum for the support teacher to give the line manager their view on whether support is being effective or not.

Promoting independence – avoiding dependency

At the heart of the work of any teacher, whether mainstream or support, lies the success of the student. However, here the success of the partnership between the mainstream teacher and support teacher is under the spotlight too.

In order for support to be effective and successful, a support teacher needs to utilize strategies and adopt measures to promote independence and avoid dependency. For example, the following scenario is a classic one of a dependency relationship being fostered. A support teacher works with an individual student; the student finds the particular exercise stressful and difficult. In order to support the student, the teacher finds him or herself giving the answers to the student. At this point, the teacher has the needs of the student in mind, but, in effect, what they are doing is promoting a state of dependency.

A more appropriate strategy would have been to start at the point where the student finds it difficult and then to move in logical steps, explaining along the way, allowing the student to see the progression and steps involved in reaching the answers required. Providing the answers gives a 'quick fix' in the short term, but gives back a false sense of achievement in the long term.

Another example of a culture of dependency is that which can exist in the relationship between the support teacher and the mainstream teacher. If we look at the case of the specialist ESOL support teacher, for example, the mainstream teacher might see anything concerned with a language focus being solely the responsibility of the support teacher. What happens then when the support teacher is unavoidably absent? What tends to take place is that the lesson has a distinct lack of cohesion either in the support received by some students who require focused support or the language element of the lesson may not be approached in a positive manner because the mainstream teacher does not see it as their 'responsibility'.

Bourne and McPake (1991) state that the best way of avoiding this is to be present at the planning stage and have an input then. By being present, the support teacher is not only providing support to the students who need it, but is also providing support to the teacher – the intention is that the mainstream teacher is skilled up along the way and ultimately the independence of the mainstream teacher is promoted.

At this point also it is worth mentioning that it is the role of the department and the individual leading it to ensure that the department is vocal within the educational establishment. All too often, the work done by the department is overlooked purely because it is carried out in isolation. An ideal way of overcoming this is by having a regular slot at staff training events. This not only demystifies the work; it also opens up dialogue with departments that have not traditionally been seen as accessible to support work or inclined to seek it.

Evaluating support – not being afraid to change

If something is working well why change? Change is not being advocated for change's sake. What is being advised is an overview of the support being offered. There is a tendency for individuals and departments to become comfortable within their roles. As already mentioned, support becomes a matter of history, namely the statement most likely to be reiterated is 'it's always been done that way'. Green (1999) argues, however, that in order for the students' best needs to be met, reviews need to take place in order to ascertain the success of the targeted support. So how should support be evaluated? Regardless of the methods adopted, the following should form the basis of any questions:

- Students need to have an input in any evaluation process. Often they are overlooked in any review of the support process. At a time when students are increasingly asked to take part in the target-setting process, then it can only be regarded as a positive measure to involve them in the evaluation.
- Any evaluation needs data, whether qualitative or quantitative – have the targets set for students been met? If not, why not? If yes, were they ambitious enough? Are there other factors that need to be taken into consideration?

- What is the mainstream teacher's opinion of the support process? It is important to note here that this does not concern personalities and neutral language should be used. This way, if criticism is forthcoming, it is the *process* rather than the individual providing the support that faces it.
- Similarly, what is the support teacher's opinion? Has support been as effective as they hoped? What did they think worked particularly well? This is the time when comparisons with the support that takes place in other departments can be made. If support has worked particularly well with another department and not with this one, this is the time to examine why.
- Now is the time to bring out the documentation and data that support teachers should have been encouraged to keep. This provides the basis for the real evaluation and gives external bodies the key information they require.

Who supports the support staff?

Thomas (1992) states that working as a support teacher is a rewarding role, but that often the needs of the teacher are overlooked. In order for support staff to feel their professional needs are being met, the following areas should form the basis of any discussion regarding how best to support them:

- Access to good quality training is important – this can be internal or external. Support staff, like other members of staff, need to keep their skills up to date. As support staff often work part time, they tend to 'miss out' on the training that others take for granted. This training can be either internal or provided via an external source, as is increasingly the case, or both.
- Attendance at staff meetings should be encouraged. The support teacher often finds him or herself 'slipping through the net' of communications. They might work across two or even three sites; therefore, decisions need to be made as to which meeting should be attended. If not, they tend to miss out on vital pieces of information regarding students, other members of staff, etc. Staff

meetings in this case are those that concern the whole support department, but also departments for which support is provided. It is not feasible to advise that the support teacher attends every meeting for every department they support, but efforts should be made to attend at least one or two per term, in order to stay 'in the loop' of communications.

- A 'buddy' system should be in place within the department for the support teacher. This provides an opportunity for each of these individuals to access the support that another professional gives. It is not over-dramatic to state that sometimes the opportunity another individual provides to listen can be the difference between someone remaining in employment or not.

- A mentoring scheme needs to be in place for all new staff – preferably from outside the department. This should last for at least a year but can also be continued if the parties involved find they benefit from it. It is important for the mentor to be located outside the department so that loyalties do not appear to be tested and issues of confidentiality are not raised.

- External links with other institutions should be encouraged. It is useful for individuals to see how others operate in a similar capacity. Often these links provide the catalyst for innovative practices to emerge.

Conclusions

For some teachers, having an additional (or several) member/s of staff in their classroom will be an uncomfortable and daunting experience. However, in order for a professional relationship to exist, line managers need to have in place strategies and structures designed to provide effective support for students. It is only then that mainstream staff will feel they are receiving support from highly skilled individuals. At the same time, it is only when support staff feel that their expertise is valued that finally students will receive high-quality, effective support which will allow them to succeed and achieve their potential.

5 Gender

It might be helpful to start by clarifying the distinction that is conventionally made between sex and gender. The former generally refers to those biological characteristics that differentiate males from females, while the latter refers to differences that are socially constructed and often taken for granted as 'natural' in society, although they are acquired through socialization and conditioning and may vary from culture to culture. The focus of this chapter will be concerned with gender and the way in which males and females learn about their roles influences and the directions they take in their lives. It will also be concerned with the way in which those working in post-compulsory education might challenge systems and practices that limit their opportunities by developing strategies that value difference and create spaces for inclusion and diversity.

In contrast to awareness about the lack of inclusion as a result of race/ethnicity and disability, gender inequalities sometimes attract less attention nowadays. The struggles of early feminism are often accepted as having already successfully achieved equality for women and girls. While there is no doubt that much about the status of women in the UK has changed, the national statistics presented in the Equal Opportunities Commission's (EOC) annual booklet, 'Facts about women and men in Great Britain' provide a very different picture.

With specific regard to education and training, it would seem that the differences between women's and men's experiences start at school, where girls now outperform boys in terms of the number of GCSEs, A levels and equivalent qualifications achieved. However, there are clear differences in subjects selected. For example, 59 per cent of girls and 48 per cent of boys gain five or more GCSE grades A*–C or equivalent and 43 per cent of girls and 34 per cent of boys gain two or more A levels or equivalent qualifications (EOC 2004a).

In terms of the subjects selected at GCSE, where English and Mathematics are prescribed by the National Curriculum, the entries in accordance with expectations are reasonably balanced between girls and boys, but where choice becomes a factor at A level/Higher, subjects selected become more segregated. For example, 70 per cent of girls opt for English Literature and Social Studies at these higher levels, as opposed to 76 per cent of boys taking Physics (DfES 2004).

This sexual stereotyping of subject choices is also particularly marked in many sectors of Modern Apprenticeships, with some of the most female-dominated sectors being early years care and education, hairdressing and social care, while plumbing, construction and the electro-technical sectors are almost entirely made up of males (LSC 2004).

Historical background of the development of rights for women in Britain

It was in 1866 that the first petition demanding voting rights for women by early suffragettes was presented to Parliament. This was followed by changes in the law, such as the Married Women's Property Act in 1882, whereby a woman became entitled to retain her property on marriage, and in 1893 when she was able to vote for and be represented on county councils. In 1918, women of 25 years of age secured the right to vote: the age for men was 21. In 1919, women were enabled to be elected as Members of Parliament and their right of entry into the professions was established. The first woman cabinet minister, Margaret Bondfield, was appointed in 1923, but it was only in 1928 that full and equal voting rights in the UK were achieved.

After the Second World War, a Royal Commission in 1946 recommended equal pay should apply in teaching, local government and the civil service, but it took until 1970 and the Equal Pay Act (EPA) before this became statutory. This was followed by the Sex Discrimination Act (SDA) in 1975, which enshrined equal pay for equal work in the law and formal discrimination against women in most other occupations was abolished. The appointment of Margaret Thatcher as the first woman prime minister in 1979 allowed some to proclaim that equality had at last been achieved but there were many who remained unconvinced and even critical of her contribution to the role of women in society.

Legislation

The EPA and SDA constitute the major legislation to ensure the practice of equal opportunities in terms of gender. The EPA was set up to ensure that an individual would enjoy a right to the same contractual pay and benefits as another individual of the opposite sex in the same employment where both were doing:

- like work; or
- work rated as equivalent under an analytical job evaluation study; or
- work that is proved to be of equal value.

Claims under the EPA are generally heard in an employment tribunal and may be brought at any time during employment or within six months of leaving employment. Successful claimants will be entitled to:

- the same level of pay or benefits as the person compared;
- backpay representing the difference in pay (subject to a limit), with interest.

If, however, the employer can prove that any difference in pay or benefits is genuinely due to a reason other than one related to sex, then the employer will not be required to provide the same pay and benefits.

Under the SDA, discrimination against individuals in the areas of employment, education and the provision of goods, facilities and services and in the disposal or management of premises on the grounds of sex was prohibited. Sex discrimination may be described as:

- direct, when an individual (woman or man) is treated less

favourably than a person of the opposite sex in comparable circumstances because of his or her sex, including, for example, sexual harassment or treating a woman adversely because she is pregnant;

- indirect, where a practice is applied to both sexes, but adversely affects a considerably larger proportion of one sex than the other. For example, an unnecessary requirement to be under 5'10" is likely to discriminate against most men or a requirement to work full time might discriminate against most women who are involved in childcare.

The creation of the EOC under the SDA was to establish a public, independent body which would monitor issues of equality between the sexes and work towards eliminating sex discrimination in the UK. In addition to challenging cases of inequality in court, the EOC has conducted research, presented information about its findings and supported employers and organizations to understand and implement its Codes of Practice. In May 2005 the Department for Trade and Industry invited consultation on their proposals for equality and diversity to extend the application of the SDA and ultimately to unify the individual commissions for race, disability and sex into a single equality and human rights body, but it is likely that this will take some time.

These two Acts are further supported by a raft of other Acts covering many aspects of women's working lives and conditions, such as the Disability Discrimination Act (1995), Employment Act (2002) on Flexible Working Regulations, the Employment of Equality (Religion or Belief) Regulations and Sexual Orientation Regulations (2003), Health and Safety at Work, etc. Act (1974), Part-time Workers (Prevention of Less Favourable Treatment) Regulations (2000), Pensions Act (1995), Race Relations Act (1976), Working Time Regulations (1998), National Minimum Wage Regulations (1999), Human Rights Act (1998) and many others. In addition, UK tribunals and courts must, where possible, interpret domestic law in accordance with the laws of the European Union (EU).

Practice

From the volume of legislation described above, it must be obvious that governments of all persuasions since the 1970s have taken the position of equality between the sexes very seriously and have demonstrated a commitment to securing it, so that it might be appropriate at this point to consider how effectively the policies have been translated into practice.

Statistics show that nearly half the people in work in the UK are women (46 per cent), but their hours of work and the jobs they work at are different. For example, nearly half of working women (44 per cent) are in part-time employment, while one in ten men work part-time (ONS 2004c). In addition, the average hourly paid earnings for women working full time are 18 per cent lower than those of men working full time. Average hourly paid earnings for women working part time are 40 per cent lower than those of men working part time (the gender pay gap differs between various jobs, with the largest gap of 44 per cent being in the banking, insurance and pension provision sector) (ONS 2004a).

This is known as the 'gender pay gap'. It is defined as the percentage difference in hourly earnings between average women's and men's earnings. It has sometimes been simplistically understood as 'a man and a woman doing the same job and receiving unequal wages' (*Guardian*, 7 September 2005) when, in fact, according to Margaret Prosser (2005), there are three factors sustaining the gender pay gap, namely:

- part-time working
- occupational segregation
- women's labour market issues, such as childcare.

All of these factors act as barriers to women's chances of entering and progressing in the workplace. The government has pledged to introduce a public sector duty to promote gender equality by December 2006, acting on the recommendations of the report to be published by the Women and Work Commission under the leadership of Prosser.

With reference to the gender stereotyping noticed in subject

choices at A level/Highers earlier, there is a parallel manifes-
tation in terms of employment occupations, reflected as:

- more than four-fifths of skilled tradespeople and process,
  plant and machine operatives are men
- four-fifths of workers in administrative, secretarial occupations and personal service jobs are women
- women hold the majority of jobs in the education, social
  work and health service sectors
- men hold the majority of jobs in transport, storage,
  communication and construction.

(ONS 2004b)

Similarly, in public and political life, although women make up
46 per cent of the labour market, they are under-represented in
positions of power and influence – only 18 per cent of the
Members of Parliament are women (House of Commons 2004)
and 24 per cent of Members of the European Parliament are
women (European Parliament 2005).

Other factors such as race, ethnicity, age and disability also
have an effect on working patterns, for example:

- in all age groups, a higher percentage of women than men
  work part time
- disabled women and men have much lower employment
  rates than non-disabled people
- in 2001, ethnic minority women and men experienced
  higher rates of unemployment than their white counter-
  parts.

(ONS 2004b; General Register Office
for Scotland 2004)

What all these individual categories are in danger of suggesting
is that one particular factor operating in isolation may be
responsible for increasing inequality, when, in fact, the process
is much more complicated, as individuals do not define
themselves singly as either female, black, disabled, gay, aged or
Muslim. Instead, a number of these factors interact and overlap
and may work in combination to reinforce disadvantage and
inequality. The inability of women to succeed in society despite
the legislation, related policies and reviews has often been

referred to as 'the glass ceiling', which suggests that, even though there are no visible barriers to opportunities and achievement, unseen obstacles, sometimes expressed in terms of gender, race/ethnicity, disability, religion, sexual orientation or age present problems for progressing beyond certain limits.

Strategies and practices to embed diversity and inclusion

Sometimes the scale of a problem seems so vast and daunting that it spawns attitudes of powerlessness and acceptance of the status quo typified by remarks such as 'that's the way of the world', 'it's always been like that and you can't change things' or 'it's part of the tradition/culture'. However, those of us involved in education also recognize it is about unlocking hidden potential in individual learners. That is sometimes sufficient to bring about changes that challenge the bigger structures and systems that have been limiting opportunities for a range of people. In considering strategies and practices to embed diversity in response to gender inequalities, the approach recommended is one that is on a small scale, manageable and realistic within constraints of what is possible in the classroom, subject/vocational area or institution in order to avoid feeling overwhelmed. Some of the statistics and information already presented might have triggered a few ideas about the stereotyping of subject areas and occupations, provision of childcare, the value of role models, and the language used in advertising and recruitment as starting points for immediate action.

Your first step might be to consider the ways in which gender operates within your subject specialism. You could base this analysis on your own observations and experience or you could check regional and national patterns. Here are just a few questions you might pose in order to highlight those aspects of your subject area that you could begin to tackle.

- How well balanced is the distribution of males and females within the group and is this reflected within the teaching team and/or in the labour market?

- How/where is information about the course/subject presented to recruit potential students?
- What kind of language is employed and at whom is it aimed?
- How might 'atypical' students be attracted to the course/subject/institution?
- What provision is there to support 'atypical' students in terms of mentors, role models, specialist equipment, additional tutoring, childcare, transport, financial assistance and so on?
- How are course demands and assessment procedures made transparent and accessible?
- Are retention rates and achievement data in terms of gender acceptable?
- What kinds of contact need to be made with those working in the vocational area within the labour market/wider society?
- What kind of staff training and development is needed to ensure gender equality?
- What are some of the implications of these questions for management within the wider institution?

Your answers should guide your next steps and help you to prioritize the order of your interventions. What you would need to do is to come up with some ideas and strategies for responding to what you have discovered. It will be more difficult if you find yourself working in isolation so make an effort to involve others, possibly including your students, in discussions. Also try to enlist the help and support of colleagues within your department/institution. It may not be possible to address everything at once, so it is advisable to set yourself manageable, realistic goals with clear end dates and work systematically towards realizing these.

At this point, it might be useful to look at more specific strategies for responding to particular examples of gender inequalities, starting with stereotyping in subject areas which leads to occupational segregation. As previously mentioned, Modern Apprenticeships demonstrate some extreme cases of stereotyping: males are largely excluded from early years, education and social care on the one hand, while on the other, they are dominant in areas such as plumbing, construction and the electro-technical sectors, which largely exclude females, in an exactly opposite way. There are a number of practical strategies set out in 'Action for Change' (EOC 2005b) in which the EOC provides advice for the Learning and Skills Councils (LSCs), using examples of various projects that might be adopted and/or modified in response to breaking down gender segregation in vocational education.

Offering workplace taster sessions, work experience and work shadowing

Gloucestershire LSC ran a project entitled, 'Does your gender make a difference?', offering hands-on experience in taster sessions to Year 10 pupils in four schools. Boys went into hairdressing, early learning and child care, while girls went into engineering and electrical installation. This was followed up with offers of work experience in the appropriate sectors. Further developments included an after-school club for girls offering engineering skills.

In another case study, a housing group applied to the LSC for European Social Fund money to run a women-only basic skills construction course called 'Changing Rooms' in Southwark, Lambeth and Croydon, targeting unemployed, black and minority ethnic women. From a total of 49 completers, 14 have passed the Construction Industry Training Board's (CITB) Construction Skills Health and Safety test and 12 have gone on to further training and employment. There are further plans to widen the scheme to make it available to more women and to run short 'taster' sessions.

Recruiting atypical trainees into different occupations

In childcare, which is not seen as a male profession, a training provider has run recruitment days in schools, targeting 14–15-year-olds and offering work experience placements in this area. They have also developed recruitment leaflets aimed specifically at males which describe the training and work experiences of other male professional childcare specialists.

Use of innovative methods, such as drama, to raise awareness among under-represented groups

Birmingham and Solihull LSC commissioned the Impact Theatre Group to improve the image of construction among young people, particularly females and ethnic minorities, by presenting a play and evaluating its impact on members of the audience. The feedback was excellent and those who attended said it had opened their eyes to the issues of being a lone female in a male training group.

In another project run by North Yorkshire LSC, a play was produced to challenge traditional attitudes and to encourage both boys and girls to consider work experience in areas they might not usually consider. In addition, following the performance people who worked in 'non-stereotypical' jobs were available to talk to the young people and answer questions. From this, the LSC believes that the play has had an impact, particularly on girls' work experience choices.

Providing labour market information

Coventry and Warwickshire LSC has produced a computer disk that sets out labour market forecasts for 2003–10, featuring a diverse range of young people on the disk envelope. Hertfordshire LSC has devised a website that displays relevant information about regional job trends and charting these job trends by occupation until 2008, as well as giving information about the qualifications required and average pay levels for different occupations.

This kind of information enables young people to make informed career choices based on future prospects for pay and progression by providing them with up-to-date labour market intelligence in a clear and accessible format.

Conclusions

This chapter has traced the development of gender (in)equality in the context of the UK since the nineteenth century. It has highlighted the way in which legislation after the Second World War and in the 1970s was aimed at resolving differences between genders in the workplace, some of which might have arisen as a result of stereotyped educational experiences and opportunities. Although much has been achieved, it has also led to feelings of complacency in many, so the ideal of gender equality remains elusive. Various strategies have been indicated to provide examples of ways in which gender inequalities in the post-compulsory education sector might be tackled. While these present ongoing challenges, the complex relationship between education and society in effecting change needs to be recognized. Does education lead to change or does it merely mirror the way in which society operates?

Rather than attempting to pursue answers to that question at this point, it would be more appropriate to reiterate the original intention of this chapter, which was to highlight issues of gender inequality and the way in which they might impact upon life choices. This reminds those of us working in post-compulsory education of the importance of valuing difference and adopting practical strategies to create opportunities for inclusion and diversity.

6 Attending to emotions and behaviour in the FE classroom

To attend: to be present; to give care; to follow; to wait upon, serve.

(*Collins Dictionary* 2003)

Emotions – why bother?

Emotions are, as Ledoux (1998) reminds us, 'at once obvious and mysterious' – so what business do they have with the job of teaching in busy FE colleges? Let's start in the present: consider for a moment how you are feeling as you read these words. Are you tired, relaxed, bored, or thinking about what to have for dinner? (Irritated by the question, perhaps?)

Whatever emotional state you are in will of course influence what you get from the next few pages and, in the same way, your students' emotional disposition profoundly influences their learning. Instinctual feelings affect, for example, students' ability to express interest in the topic you are teaching, to concentrate, deal with difficulties, to achieve and to celebrate achievements as and when they happen. Emotions are a continuous thread in education and yet, as teachers, we sometimes fail to give them the time, attention and thought they deserve.

Morris (1991) puts the case succinctly: '. . . to view education as essentially an affair of intellectual development . . . hopelessly underestimates the extent to which intellectual achievement and the very possibility of rationality itself are intimately bound up with the ordering of emotional life'. Despite this, our educational system continues to operate as if emotions were somehow separable from the intellect. The ages of 14–19 are important years during which, among other things, we negotiate puberty, discover the fallibility of parents and other adults and begin to define our sexual and social preferences.

Nothing less than independence and a separate adult identity are at stake. And yet, at the same time as this sometimes scary, sometimes exciting but always difficult development is going on, teenagers are pressed into taking life-defining vocational and academic decisions based on exams, coursework and interviews. The pressure on parents, teachers and students can be enormous.

One consequence of this pressure can be that, as teachers, we only notice emotions when they become a problem in the classroom in the form of 'bad behaviour'. It is, of course, true that when a student becomes tearful, withdrawn or behaves in a confrontational way, we need to respond quickly to their needs. However, if we only think about emotions at the point when they manifest as 'difficult' behaviour, we run the risk of simply reacting to situations rather than responding to them constructively. When this happens, we make more work for ourselves and, occasionally, make already tricky classroom problems worse. Therefore, the purpose of this chapter is to help you think about the role of emotions in learning before you have to deal with the sharp end of their expression. How, as teachers, can we think about our own and our students' emotions? What constitutes good practice in working with this, essentially personal, realm of experience in the classroom? First, a brief word about where emotions come from – what gives them their 'obvious and mysterious' quality?

The origins of emotion

From a biological point of view, emotions derive from primordial responses to danger. The need to survive hostile living conditions among our ancestors led to the development of finely tuned nerve impulses in the brain and body that alert us to threat. This is generally described as the 'fight or flight' response and was first proposed by Walter Cannon in the 1920s. According to this theory, in an emergency situation, energy is directed to muscles which are needed to maintain our survival. If we are, for example, being chased, energy is directed via the blood to large and powerful muscles in our legs and arms and away from internal organs. The sensations we experience such as a pounding heart, sweaty palms and tense muscles are those we may label as fear. In this sense, emotions have a strong physical dimension as well as a more consciously processed reality. This physical dimension can have an irresistible quality. We speak of being 'in the grip' of an emotion, meaning that we feel somehow forced to act in one way or another. It is precisely because emotions have this compelling quality that we need the space and means to think about our own and our students' emotional experiences.

When we try to make sense of emotions we use cognition. Cognitive processes include things like information, memory and context. For example, in the right context, sensations such as a pounding heart, sweaty palms and dry mouth can be understood as signalling desire or excitement rather than fear. The point is, of course, that emotions are not entirely about sensation, they are an elaborate interplay of physical, social and mental processes. Understanding this interplay is not straightforward.

Two approaches for understanding emotions in the classroom

There are a variety of approaches to thinking about emotions and their role in learning. Two contrasting sets of ideas stand out which we can refer to as behavioural and psychodynamic models. In this section, I will describe the main features of each and the potential consequences for dealing with emotions in the classroom. The aim in doing this is not to make finite judgements about which approach is best. Rather, it is to point out that, whether or not we are aware of it, we tend to favour one approach over another in our teaching. The approach we favour leads us to think about, question and act on emotions in the classroom in very different ways.

Behaviourism – a model about 'doing'

Behavioural theories originated in the animal experiments of Pavlov. His observations led him to develop the idea that behaviour could be conditioned by the appropriate use of stimuli and response. So, in educational terms, if a teacher smiles and says good morning to her class regularly enough, she provides stimuli the students will come to expect. In response, many will also smile and greet the teacher. Social psychologists such as Skinner and Bandura elaborated the stimulus–response theory to include the concept of 'reinforcement'. A reinforcer is anything that increases and strengthens a desirable response. For example, giving written work a good grade, verbal praise and encouragement will increase feelings of worth and increase the likelihood of a student repeating the behaviour that led to the reward.

In many ways, the ideas of behaviourism have become accepted commonsense practice in teaching. Doubtless, it is nothing new to be reminded that positive comments are helpful in encouraging learning and conformity within a class – these ideas are taught to us all in the course of teacher training. However, I would argue that it's worth looking at these deceptively simple ideas more deeply. If as a teacher you work behaviourally with your students, you are making a key assumption about emotions. This assumption is that emotions are, in essence, nothing more than ways of behaving. These ways of behaving can, in turn, be influenced positively or negatively by your behaviour. A teacher's role is to manage learning and maintain authority and order. Conflict, as and when it arises, is a problem to be dealt with as effectively as possible, using rewards and possibly punishments to bring about solutions. Ultimately, the business of teaching is to impart rational knowledge. In doing this, you will prefer to ignore the origins and meanings of 'irrational' emotions and deal solely with their consequences. Outbursts of emotion in the classroom are a result of poor learning in the arena of self-control; as far as possible your role is to challenge and correct this. As a teacher you will be observant in your classroom. From this perspective, the question 'What's going on?' is all about what can be seen to be happening in the class. It will include things such as whether and how people participate in the lesson, where they sit in the room, their body language, patterns of attendance, absence and achievement. You will notice your own contributions in these respects and also will be aware of the physical climate of the classroom. Is it warm, cold, too dark, too light? You will ask questions such as, 'What works to keep my students happy and busy in the classroom? What cues do I give my students which show my interest in their learning? How can I focus on getting my students, as Bigge put it, to ". . . relate to their environment in such a way as to enhance their ability to use themselves and their environment more effectively?" ' (Bigge and Shermis 1982).

If you are keen on a behavioural approach, you are probably quite categorical about boundaries in relation to your students. For example, you are likely to have clear ideas about what constitutes a 'personal' as opposed to an 'educational' problem for your students. You will probably want to refer 'personal' problems to college counsellors rather than try to deal with them in the classroom. This way of dealing with difficulties certainly has advantages. One of them is that students are likely to know where they stand with you and what they can expect. You will, nonetheless, always be willing to be pragmatic and to try different behaviour on different groups. 'What works' to help your groups settle and concentrate makes for 'good enough' practice.

If, however, tried and tested behavioural techniques fail, it may be time to look at situations and relationships afresh.

Psychodynamics – a model about 'thinking'

This approach applies insights from counselling and psycho-analysis to education. Unlike behaviourism, a psychodynamic approach puts emotions at the centre of learning. This is because effective learning always involves making personal meaning out of abstract information. For example, we feel happy, sad or indignant at the fates of those we study in history or literature. We feel enriched by learning IT skills and enjoy and marvel at the patterns of numbers revealed in mathematics. If ideas fail to become personalized in this way, education is reduced to a chore of pointless rote learning. It may become merely '. . . a demand which invites either a spurious com-pliance or a rebellious subversion' (Coren 1997).

For a student to make the leap into personal meaning, the

relationship between teacher and students is crucial. New ideas and possibilities can be threatening and the wise teacher recognizes that internal conflict is sometimes a necessary element of learning and growth. Seen from this perspective, the teacher's role is to enter a broadly helping relationship with the student. In 1951, Carl Rogers suggested the role of the counsellor may provide a model for some crucial aspects of this relationship:

> 'If the creation of an atmosphere of acceptance, understanding and respect is the most effective basis for facilitating the learning which is called therapy, then might it not be the basis for the learning which is called education?' (Rogers 1951, p. 384)

In other words, who you are in the classroom and the extent to which you convey genuine interest in, understanding of, and respect for your students has a vital effect on their learning. Seeking solutions to problems is not always, from this point of view, the most helpful thing a teacher can do. Listening, questioning and supporting students in finding their own solutions to problems is more important.

Salzberger-Wittenberg, Henry and Osborne (1983) argue that it is helpful to think of the teacher–student relationship as mirroring that of a parent and child. Just as growing up involves learning to tolerate lots of uncertainties, fears and anxieties, so does learning at school and college. (If this seems far-fetched, take a minute to remember the anxieties you had when you began training as a teacher. You probably wondered if you would be good enough to cope with the classroom. You may have panicked about whether you knew enough of your subject. You might have worried about how you appeared to your students and new colleagues. Did they think you were any good? Were you better or worse than they were?) Just as a good parent will understand and tolerate the tantrums and tears of a child without being vengeful, sarcastic or dismissive, a good teacher will tolerate and listen to the anxieties of their students. In doing so, they will convey the message that anxiety and fear cannot overwhelm the student, rather that they can and will cope.

A teacher working from this perspective is likely to be interested in what lies at the root of behaviour. They are aware that previous experiences as well as future hopes and fears affect what goes on in a class. They try to be conscious of their own personal stresses and strains and are aware of how these might affect their students. Generally, they are happy to share some elements of their personal life with their students and there is evidence (e.g. Harkin 2002) that this is an important factor in teenage student satisfaction with teachers. They work collaboratively rather than trying to resolve problems like a manager. In seeking students' opinions about problems, they model ways of thinking and reflection and provide a shared language for tacit emotional expression. For example, 'Every Monday in this class I notice a lot of agitation and talking over me. Has anyone else noticed it? What's going on here do you think?' Empathic phrases are used to show the teacher appreciates that students have their own points of view and interpretations of events. 'Some of you might be feeling a bit overwhelmed by all the paperwork I've just handed out. Am I right? What can we do about that?'

At its best this kind of thoughtful dialogue engenders a virtuous cycle of trust and respect. A high level of social interest and shared control allows individuals to relax. They can focus on learning the subject rather than defending their own space and status in the classroom.

Attending to emotions, some dos and don'ts

Previously, I contrasted a behavioural approach as being about 'doing' with a psychodynamic one, concerned with 'thinking'. This is, of course, a matter of emphasis rather than exact distinction. As teachers, we need to reflect as well as take action in the classroom. To this end I would argue we should always be open to new ideas, wherever they come from.

There are, nonetheless, some underlying principles in attending to emotions which will serve you well whatever else you do with your students. They are:

- Do take some time to notice the 'emotional climate' of

your classes. How is the morale of your students? How do you and the group handle conflict and dissent? What, in particular, are the beginning and end of classes like?

- When teaching teenagers, remember that adolescence is a time of growth and, therefore, insecurity. College can be threatening as well as liberating because it demands change. What are we asking people to give up when they come to our classes and what are we offering them in return?

- Most difficult emotions which upset classes are not deliberately chosen by students as a way of creating disruption. They arise when they do for many reasons, some of which may have more to do with the student's internal reality than the external classroom. Therefore, always respect feelings, however inappropriate they may appear to you.

- Do not feel forced to react to emotionally charged situations. Unless there is direct danger to life and limb, very little needs a lightning response. Take time to reflect and think before responding. It can be helpful to you and your students to tell them you are taking thinking time: it means you value them and your relationship with them.

- Where appropriate and possible, include students in your reflections about emotions in the classroom. Don't shy away from asking students hard questions. For example, 'What are you afraid of?' to the long-time work avoider, or 'How do you think I feel when . . .' are both potentially useful questions if timed correctly.

- Finally, attending to emotions is a skill worth developing not only for your students but for your own benefit. The educationalist Frank Smith (2005) reminds us that '. . . teachers who get 'burned out' are not the ones who are constantly learning, which can be exhilarating, but those who feel they must stay in control and ahead of the students all the time'. Is it possible that the beauty of attending to emotions is that we can never be in full control? Emotions ebb and flow and, like waves, the skill is not to try and tame them but to learn to ride them.

7 Younger students in FE

First the bad news: 'I didn't come into further education to teach 14–16-year-olds. They're just too young for college. They're only the ones the schools don't want. They see college as one big bunk off from school and what can I do with them when they're only here one day a week? Other staff raise their eyebrows when they see my timetable. Why do I – a new member of staff – get them? It's not fair.'

These are just a few of the worries you may have teaching younger students for the first time and some of these concerns are valid. Fourteen to sixteen-year-olds coming into college from school can stand out from the rest of the students. Their status in the social hierarchy may be low, their behaviour based on experiences at school rather than college, and their attitude sometimes reluctant. Nevertheless, this group are an increasing cohort within our sector. In 2004, it was estimated that over 100,000 students of this age were being taught in FE colleges (*The Times Educational Supplement*, 13 February 2004), and the signs are that this figure will rise steeply in the next few years as more colleges form reciprocal teaching arrangements with schools. The good news is that younger students can be fun to teach, enthusiastic and rewarding. Many reports testify to the students' enthusiasm for FE compared to school: 'You don't just sit there and work. You can get up and move and there are more ways of doing things . . . The way teachers speak to you is different' (LSDA and Oxford Brookes University 2004). Likewise, for teachers, the difference can be inspiring: 'It can be hard teaching younger ones, but it's great when I see that some get a lot out of it' (FE teacher 2004). You will considerably broaden your own skills and CV as a result of teaching a younger age group. And, let's face it, during the course of your career, you will probably teach some far less mature adults than the teenagers in this group!

The vast majority of students you may be called upon to teach will be in the 14–16 age range. Nomenclature, like status, is tricky with this group – are they pupils, students, children, young adults? For the purposes of this chapter, they will be referred to as 'younger students'. The aim of this chapter is to help you think about younger students in a constructive way. The chapter also aims to help you confront and reflect on some of the concerns you may have about including them in your teaching, and to help you ask the right questions of your workplace in order to better deal with the wider context of teaching this group.

Younger students – who, when and where?

Arrangements vary but, typically, 14–16-year-olds come into college through three avenues. Some 'infill' traditional academic courses because the subject they want to take is not available at school. In this instance, one or two individuals may attend classes alongside older students. They probably have strong motivation, are reasonably high achievers and fit in easily with the majority of the class.

Other young students attend as a class for whole days and occasionally for weekly blocks. They follow a discrete timetable, bringing learning mentors and/or teachers with them. These students may well have additional educational needs and, in parts of the country where these exist, may be from special schools.

A third group are the vocational part-time attendees. These students are at college because they are unlikely to achieve many passes in traditional GCSE or A/S subjects. They are sent to college in order to give them the opportunity to learn useful vocational skills. For example, they may be taking courses in catering, brick-laying or hairdressing. At the time of writing, this is a fast-growing arrangement supported by the development of new vocational diplomas. Many colleges now offer, in partnership with schools, a vocational curriculum for large numbers of younger students in their locality.

It may be surmised from the above that younger students tend to be concentrated at either end of the educational spectrum. They are the academic achievers at one end and the less academic working on practical subjects at the other, with all the difficulties that these two groups can bring. Before we look at the likely educational needs of these groups in more detail, there is one important factor about younger students in further education that needs consideration. This is, quite simply, that most attend college on a part-time basis.

The ramifications of part-time status

Many younger students, regardless of what they are studying, come to college for just one or two days each week. This has social and educational ramifications for them and you, their lecturer. Building rapport can take longer than you expect and because 'belonging' is a process, be prepared for new students to take time to trust their new environment. Colleges are almost always bigger than schools and operate on a different social scale than that which younger learners are used to. All of us experience some disorientation in new places and may 'wish to draw close boundaries so as to feel less exposed' (Salzberger-Wittenberg, Henry and Osborne 1983). Being aware of this and watching out for new younger learners is a part of your role as an adult figure in this (for them) new, strange environment. It is normal for them to test the teacher, challenge authority and jostle for position within a new environment. The fact that students are in college one or two days a week may well mean that what is sometimes characterized as a group 'storming' phase goes on for several weeks (Tuckman 1965).

During a 'storming' period, your role is to be a consistent adult presence who is seen to be fair and focused on encouraging educational achievement. Having an activity early on in your teaching which leads to recognized and certificated achievement in whatever subject younger students are learning will help in this respect. Being clear early in the year about classroom rules and their application is also vital. Explicit rules make for explicit expectations and allow sanctions to be applied in a way that is seen to be fair by the students.

Nevertheless, even with your best efforts, younger students may feel only a tangential attachment to the college. In practical terms, they miss out on enrichment opportunities such as clubs and outings that, for example, a student union can provide. Many look physically diminutive compared to older students and can feel awkward about being in a more adult environment than school. Even those who appear to blend more easily with the aged 16-plus cohort will have to negotiate two cultures: that of school, which, to date, has formed their educational experiences and expectations, and that of college, which is new and uncharted territory.

Cultural differences between school and college

There are significant differences between school and college and younger students come to college with the dominant culture of school in their heads. To appreciate how they might think and feel about the transition to college, it is important that you, in turn, think about these differences. These can be described as the Three Rs – differences in Rules, Relationships and Roles.

Firstly, rules. School rules are explicit, non-negotiable and liable to be publicly enforced. Lining up outside classrooms, wearing the correct uniform, pushing chairs under desks, using the canteen at specific times according to year groups: all these are examples of typical school rules. They have a dual purpose: to create order and to be seen to be sustaining that order, so in this sense, rules at school are for their own sake.

Contrast this with your own college rules. What do you notice? You will probably spot that there are fewer rules and those that exist are more likely to be tacit and negotiable. For example, most lecturers are happy to be called by their first name. Standards of behaviour in the corridors and public spaces are likely to be kept by consensus rather than enforcement. There are no uniforms and, of course, no bells to signal the start and end of classes. At a deeper level, this reflects the fact that the ethos of college is not the same as that of school. Even if younger students at your college are educated on discrete courses and housed in separate areas, they will still, to some extent, have to adjust to this new environment. Initially, they may feel insecure and uncertain of their surroundings.

As well as learning to deal with new rules, younger students also have to adjust to new relationships within college. They will have been the experienced 'old hands' at school, but in college they have to negotiate a new and looser set of relationships. 'Forming new relationships can be problematic ... Young people at this stage are caught between a drive towards independence and a need for guidance. They value the more adult teacher–student relationship that colleges offer, but many lack the maturity to make that kind of experience work – possibly as a result of previous learning experiences' (Harkin 2004). Furthermore, in college they may occupy a low status, but ironically, and confusingly, age is not in itself a status indicator at college. Hierarchies are harder to decipher at college than school and younger students experience a challenge to find how they 'fit in'. Working relationships need to be formed with a wider range of people than they have been used to at school; for example, older students, adult students, lecturers, support staff and managerial staff.

This brings us to the last of the three 'Rs'; namely, roles. In school, roles are, by and large, very distinct. Teachers are the gatekeepers of rules and there is an expectation that pupils will obey. Lessons are driven by external assessments in the form of SATS and achievements are closely tracked. In colleges we do not, of course, work to the National Curriculum, so external assessments are less pressing. There is space for some discussion and negotiation about when and how assessments take place. In general, role distinctions are more blurred and responsibilities are shared more than in schools. Ask yourself: 'Who takes responsibility for lessons, learning and discipline in your class?' It is likely that you do not see this as your job alone and, indeed, it is a purpose of college to encourage maturity by sharing decisions with students. Whereas full-time students change their habits to fit in with college expectations, part-time younger students have to learn to play and manipulate two roles – that of the pupil at school and the student at college.

In essence, we need to appreciate that the social demands

college places on younger students can be complicated. A new start at college can be an opportunity to break free of old school roles and relationships. The classroom clown may want to be taken seriously, but the hard worker may be afraid they will be seen as a 'boffin' by their classmates. Students will ask questions of themselves, but these will rarely be verbally articulated. 'Who am I in this place? Where do I fit? Can I be the same or different from when I am at school? What if I try and change – what are the benefits and risks?'

What can we do? The teacher's role

So far, I have tried to sketch out some of the key reasons why younger learners can find college a difficult as well as exciting environment to which to adjust. What can we do as teachers to help them deal with this adjustment? How can we minimize the effect of the barriers they face in settling into college? Are there special rules we should follow when teaching groups of 14–16-year-olds?

Firstly, do some background work on younger students before they come to college. This is an essential investment to offset possible problems later on.

- Find out about the students' school before they arrive. Visit it and get a feel for the atmosphere and ethos. Is the school relaxed and based on co-operation between pupils and staff? Is it authoritarian, with power and decision making concentrated in the hands of staff? Is it author-itative and somewhere between those two extremes? Knowing this can help you develop an idea of how the students will perceive college, your teaching and their learning. It also identifies you with the school and you will represent some continuity between school and college.
- Can you be given the time and facility to observe classes at school? This can be invaluable help in understanding the educational culture your students come from and the type of teaching and learning they are used to.
- Ask about the students' official school records but, as importantly, find out about how they see their time at

school. In order to do this, you will need to interview them. This practice varies from college to college. Some have diagnostic interviews to assess younger students' strengths and areas of need. Others will have selective interviewing which will allow you to accept or reject particular students before they start college.

- Listen carefully to what students tell you at interview. This means listening to the type of words they use as well as the overall sense of what they are saying. Do they have hope for their future? Can you sense if they have internal authority or do they rely on being told what to do and how to do things? How positively or negatively do they assert their wants and wishes? What are they not telling you? (Ask them what they think their teachers would say about them if they were asked. You might be surprised at the frankness of many of the replies you will get!)

Once your younger students are in college there are several things you can do which will support you all.

- Ask your line manager for advice on health and safety precautions in your classroom. Your common-law 'duty of care' is higher for under-16s than it is for older students. Depending on the subject you are teaching and the equipment involved, you may need extra staff or different provisions for supervising and checking work in the classroom.
- For the under-16s, education is compulsory so it is important that your college is clear about lines of responsibility. Ask your line manager what the contractual arrangements are between school, college and the local education authority for younger students. Where are they officially enrolled? Who is responsible for attendance and following up unauthorized absences? Are younger students allowed out of the building during breaks and lunchtimes? What are the arrangements in case of emergencies or sudden college closures?
- Don't panic about *how* to teach younger students. In many respects, they are not substantially different from the older teenagers you teach every day. Teachers who have been

successfully teaching this group for years offer the following advice: 'Do as you do'; 'Just be extra sensitive to their needs and accentuate the positives'. 'A good teacher can teach a variety of ages and good teachers will manage all sorts of classes.'

- Finally, remember that coming to college can be of great benefit for younger students, although recent evidence (LSDA and Oxford Brookes University 2004) shows that, initially, their experience of college is ambivalent. The decision to attend college is often made for schoolchildren and they perceive that the less academic are the ones who are selected. However, once in college, they may find that they really enjoy it and believe they are learning more than at school.

Younger students can offer a great opportunity to enjoy what FE has traditionally prided itself on. You may rediscover one of the reasons you went into FE teaching – to provide a second chance.

8 Dyslexia

What is dyslexia?

There has been much controversy recently over the existence of dyslexia. In the past, it has been called a middle-class excuse for failing children and professionals still argue about the definition. However, despite its bad press, dyslexia does exist and affects many people; I spent over 12 years in an inner city college diagnosing and supporting dyslexic adults and have seen the difference early diagnosis and support has made to many students.

Dyslexia is also known as a specific learning difficulty (SpLD) and is a phonological difficulty with processing language, usually associated with reading and spelling. However, it can also include a whole host of other difficulties such as handwriting, speech and organizational problems to do with sequencing. It has absolutely nothing to do with intellectual ability: in fact, many would argue that dyslexia is a gift – the ability to see things holistically and differently.

SpLD is the name most commonly used by educationalists and is used in the education acts to describe dyslexia. Dyslexia is more commonly used within medical or neurological contexts, as well as colloquially. Dyslexia is also classified as a disability by the Department for Work and Pensions (DWP).

Historical overview

Originally, dyslexia was thought to affect only reading. In 1896, Pringle Morgan coined the phrase 'word blindness' as a condition that affected some children with reading difficulties. He recognized that, for some, reading difficulties were not due to lack of concentration, stupidity or laziness. Some advances were made in the early part of the twentieth century, when eye surgeon James Hinshelwood first recognized 'congenital' word blindness. In 1925, Samuel Orton detected strephosymbia (twisting of symbols) and also gave recognition to the correlation between reading difficulties and patterns of 'handedness' and 'eyedness' (left/right dominance). Despite these advances, it was not until the latter half of the century that any real progress was made.

In 1978, the Warnock Report for Special Educational Needs, after many studies including that of Critchley (1970), acknowledged a discrepancy between academic achievement and the intelligence of a child, and dyslexia was finally recognized as syndrome. The term SpLD was encouraged as opposed to 'dyslexia', yet, ironically, dyslexic students prefer to be called 'dyslexic'. Historically, it was thought that dyslexia was due to specific processing difficulties in one side of the brain – the left hemisphere – largely due to the fact that the left hemisphere is responsible for most language processing and sequencing. Galaburda and Kemper (1979) thought that dyslexics were usually left-handed and right-brain dominant and that there was poor processing in the less dominant left hemisphere. This was based on the reasoning and findings of the psychiatrist and neurologist Samuel Orton (1937) on the correlation between speech disorders and the high incidence of left-handedness. In the vast majority of right-handed individuals, the left side of the brain is crucial or dominant in determining perceptual and speech functioning. It then followed that if this was true, impairment to the left hemisphere was responsible for dyslexia.

'. . . if, indeed, damage to the dominant half of the thinking brain is proven responsible for the loss of reading and speech ability in previously normal adults via autopsy studies – resulting in alexia and aphasia – then children failing to acquire normal reading and/or speech functioning (dyslexia and dysphasia) must have an impairment in this very same area of the brain . . .' (Levinson 2003, p. 166)

This theory is still considered to be correct explanation of the cause of dyslexia by some neurologists. However, the most dominant theories in the past few years have related to the cerebellum, a bean-shaped mass of grey and white tissue the size of a small fist sitting on the brain stem beneath the base of the skull. The cerebellum operates as 'monitor and co-ordinator of the brain's other centres and as mediator between them and the body'. Several prominent neuro-physiologists have conducted research (Llinas 1992, Fawcett and Nicolson 1992) over the past few years and agreed that the cerebellum is directly involved with other parts of the brain and has a role in dyslexia and its related symptoms.

> '... anatomical evidence and behavioural evidence combine to suggest that this enlarged cerebellum not only contributes to motor function, but also to some sensory, cognitive, linguistic and emotional aspects of behaviour.' (Leiner, Leiner and Dow 1991, p. 113)

Levinson (2003) defines dyslexia as an inner ear dysfunction due to a disorder in the cerebellum. He reports that the cerebellum has four major functions that are responsible for physical movement, fine motor tuning, awareness of space, and timing and rhythmic motions. He claims that a disorder in any or all of these areas will result in dyslexia; for example, if voluntary motor responses are 'improperly' fine-tuned, acts such as tying shoe laces, holding pens, writing and speech may be affected. These difficulties are typical for people with dyslexia.

As I have already mentioned, dyslexia is usually associated with difficulties with reading and writing, particularly spelling. However, there are many other symptoms such as poor short-term memory, disorganization, left/right confusion and a poor sense of timing. There may also be other difficulties associated with dyslexia, such as problems with numbers, handwriting and poor motor coordination.

Students may have all, or a combination of, the following 'general' symptoms:

- Generally disorganized – the student's file is always in a mess, with pieces of work missing or 'mislaid'.
- The student is often late or misses appointments because he or she has forgotten the time, place, and so forth.

- He or she may seem 'clumsy', always knocking things over or bumping into objects.
- The student avoids reading aloud in class and always takes a passive role in group discussion.
- The student has difficulty with pronunciation, particularly with multi-syllabic words.
- The student has difficulty with writing essays, although he or she appears to understand the subject during the lesson. Generally he or she is 'good' orally, but has not produced much written work and may even avoid it completely.
- The student consistently makes spelling errors, even though he or she has had those errors corrected several times.
- The student's handwriting may be messy and immature.
- The content of the student's essays may be inspiring but there is a lack of appropriate punctuation and grammar.
- The student may be a very good artist, hairdresser, musician or mechanic, but struggles to meet deadlines with assignments.

It is important that students who exhibit a combination of these symptoms are assessed quickly to enable them to receive appropriate support, as this is dependent on the type of SpLD diagnosed. There are three main types of difficulty and it is fairly common for someone to have more than one. The following list may give you an idea of the type of difficulty the student is experiencing, enabling you to revise your teaching methods accordingly. There is a boon here, as 'dyslexic-friendly' teaching methods are effective for all students.

Auditory processing difficulties

Reading
Klein (1997) suggests that students will have problems with 'holding' and discriminating sounds which results in difficulty decoding when reading. Students may read with good understanding, but will often struggle with words they do not know. They rely heavily on context and substitute whole words in

attempts to make sense. 'They usually make frequent repetitions and often self-correct.'

Spelling

Dyslexic students encounter considerable difficulty with spelling, resulting in omissions of sounds and mispronunciations, e.g. 'sreet' for 'street', 'theer' for 'three'. Sequential errors involving sound confusions are common, e.g. 'gril' for 'girl', 'fuirt' for 'fruit'.

As students with auditory processing difficulties experience problems with sounds, visual strategies should be explored. You should consider the following approaches:

- Directed activities for reading texts (DARTs) – this involves highlighting, cutting and pasting, and moving around enlarged text.
- Help learners to devise images and draw on their own to remember the look and sound of letters.
- Break words into visual patterns rather than sounds.
- Where possible, use visual images as well as text – diagrams, mind maps and spidergrams can help make important links.

Visual processing difficulties

Reading

Students often rely on a phonic approach and will make non-word substitutions, frequently showing semantic weaknesses. They will ignore punctuation, read jerkily and may miss out words or lose their place – 'jumping' lines is a common problem. They will almost certainly experience difficulty with comprehension of the text because they are trying so hard to recognize the individual words.

Spelling

They may mis-sequence the letters, particularly, for example, 'blet' for 'belt', 'trail' for 'trial' and 'aviod' for 'avoid'. They may omit endings and plurals. (If the student's first language is not English they may make similar errors and this is due to 'cultural' differences and may not necessarily be dyslexia.)

Handwriting

This may not be disordered, although there may be some confusion with b/d and p/q due to visual processing problems.
Approaches to consider:

- When writing on the board, ensure that you write clear, fairly large letters.
- Utilize the LSCWC (Look, Say, Cover, Write, Check) spelling programme using an auditory approach.
- Encourage word processing instead of handwritten work, as tapping the keys can be less stressful than trying to form well-rounded letters. The spell checks function can also help with spelling, as long as the student has an idea of the spelling of a word.
- Try to find out about specialist software, such as Dragon Dictate, that allow the student to dictate into the computer.

The following strategies are suitable for general support for reading and spelling and can be adapted for students with both auditory and visual processing difficulties:

- PQ4R (Preview, Question, Read, Reflect, Recite, Review) – learners practise previewing a text to anticipate from text features and context. Formulate questions 'to be answered' as they read. 'Read, reflect, recite, review' each paragraph or section as they read. These activities help them engage actively with the text.
- LSCWC (Look, Say, Cover, Write, Check) – an individualized programme that can be used to improve spelling. The student chooses up to ten words to be learned. A chart is used to plot their progress. This programme is designed to reinforce spelling in the short-term memory; the spellings are tried on the day and then at intervals over the following week.

Motor difficulties

Reading
The student may not have significant difficulties with reading. However, there may be difficulties with hand–eye coordination and visual tracking may be a problem.

Spelling
The student may be able to accurately spell most words phonetically. However, as handwriting relies on motor-memory, students may experience the following difficulties:

- Telescoping – they miss out the middle of words, e.g. 'beging for 'beginning'.
- Preservation – they may repeat a letter pattern, e.g. 'indivividual' for 'individual'.
- The hand 'takes over' – they substitute one word for another, e.g. 'particular' for 'peculiar'.

Handwriting
There may be quite severe handwriting difficulties; letters may be poorly formed and multi-directional. The letters may go 'off' the line and may be a mixture of lower and upper case.
Approaches to consider:

- Use discrete support to enable students to practise handwriting.
- Use kinaesthetic methods such as clay or large crayons to encourage full arm movement and reinforce the motor-memory.
- Encourage word processing.
- Where possible, encourage the students to use voice recognition technology.

Many students also struggle with mathematics. They may have a specific learning difficulty in mathematics – dyscalculia – and require specialist support, or they may experience difficulties as part of their dyslexia. They may have difficulty in reading the questions or general number reversal, e.g. 61 for 16, or have directional difficulties. These are particularly significant for adding, subtraction and multiplication. If you are supporting these students, you need to discuss their needs with the learning support coordinator.

Support

The most important contribution that you can make as a teacher is to be able to recognize possible symptoms of SpLD and ensure the student is then given appropriate support. You cannot be expected to be an expert by reading this guide *but* you can make a difference to your students by employing 'dyslexia–friendly' teaching methods. These methods will benefit all your students, not just those who are dyslexic.

9 Understanding autistic spectrum disorders

For all of my life I was the different kid.

Fred in Sainsbury, 2000

This chapter begins with a brief introduction to autism and Asperger's syndrome (AS) and makes a distinction between the two. It then presents the defining characteristics of autistic spectrum disorders with particular emphasis on AS and, finally, offers information and advice for the FE lecturer about how to teach students with autism or AS in mainstream classes in inclusive settings.

What is autism?

The term autism was coined in 1911 by the psychiatrist Eugen Bleuler to describe what he perceived as one of the key symptoms of schizophrenia – social withdrawal and active detachment. Autism literally means 'selfishism', and it is a lifelong and complex developmental disability that affects the way a person communicates, behaves and relates to people around them. The condition varies from person to person; symptoms are individual and can be considerably different. Some people with the condition have accompanying learning difficulties, while others have an average or above average IQ. In the same way, language skills may range from mute to complex grammatical speech. For these reasons, people with autism are described as being on the autistic spectrum and are commonly described as having autistic spectrum disorder (ASD). Recent figures indicate that autism affects about one in every thousand people and it occurs between four and fifteen times more frequently in males than females. When females have the disorder, they tend to have more severe symptoms and lower intelligence (National Austic Society 2001, p. 27).

What are the causes of ASDs?

The cause of autism is fiercely and openly debated in the media and popular press but at the moment there is no known or proven cause. In common with other syndromes and disorders, 'autism' is a label used to describe a range of symptoms which provide a diagnosis that helps to make sense of the defining pathological (different from the norm) features, rather than an explanation of why they occur (Jordan and Powell 1995, p. 3). The Medical Review Council's (MRC) 'Review of autism research' (2001) describes autism as 'a neurological disorder linked to the development of social and communication skills'. The existing research provides evidence that suggests people with autism have neurological underactivity in the parts of the brain which control planning and complex actions and which process social and emotional information. It is likely that a number of genes are involved, but it is not yet clear which these are. It is also probable that some environmental factors are influential, for example, mother's illness during pregnancy, childhood illness or food intolerance. The involvement of a virus or a reaction to the MMR (measles, mumps and rubella) vaccine has been categorically rejected by the MRC, although many parents still believe that there is a connection, and the controversy continues. From the available reliable evidence, it would seem that autism results from a 'cocktail' of genetic predisposition and environmental factors, but the nature of the interaction between the two is not yet clear and research continues (MRC 2001).

Background and definitions

Unfortunately, although not unusually, people on the autistic spectrum are often described using the terms of their medical or clinical diagnosis. 'He is a high-functioning autist' or 'He is Asperger's' or, worse, 'He is an Aspie!'. These labels may cause offence and they are also known to be damaging to expectations and self-esteem (Corbett 1996), and in the professional edu-cational context are best avoided. However, that said, it is crucial that teachers and lecturers have an accurate under-standing of the complexities of autism if the 'right' attitudes are to prevail and support is to be provided through the culture of true inclusion (see Chapter 1). So the following information is provided in order to understand, rather than to label or categorize.

Kanner syndrome (classic autism)

In the USA in 1943, Dr Leo Kanner used 'autism' to describe the behaviours in children who presented with childhood schizophrenia. He described the principal clinical features as: a lack of responsiveness to others; detachment from parents; absence of normal language development and speech; temper tantrums; repetitive activities; obsessiveness with small things (patterns, music, puzzles); and an insistence on the preservation of sameness in the environment (Kanner and Eisenberg 1956). There is a further distinction made in 'Kanner autism' between 'high-' and 'low-'functioning traits. High-functioning autism is generally used to describe those people who show all the symptoms of autism early in childhood (usually before the age of 3). They may have a slightly below average IQ (80–90) and an exceptional ability in one area such as music, drawing, matrix reasoning (the ability to see shapes and patterns), mathematical skills or rote memory. These abilities are known as 'islets of intelligence' (Baron-Cohen and Bolton 1993, p. 52) and people who have them have been called the 'autistic savants', the term used to describe the character played by Dustin Hoffman in *Rain Man* (1988). Low-functioning autism is generally used to describe those people who also show all the symptoms of autism in early childhood but have an IQ of less than 70. These people have severe or profound learning dis-abilities, and display all the associated characteristics in addition to the additional characteristics of autism. Commonly, they have little or no speech and display extreme behaviours such as self-harming.

Asperger's syndrome

Hans Asperger, working in Austria in 1945, gave his name to what he thought of as a personality disorder in children with similar traits who had been referred to his psychiatry department. He made a significant distinction between these children and schizophrenic patients, noting that they were not psychotic, nor did they show a disintegration of personality (Munrow 2005). AS is distinguishable from Kanner's syndrome in that those with AS have mild symptoms of autism, an average or above average IQ, and have no delay in language or cognitive development (World Health Organisation 1992). The two defining characteristics of individuals who have AS are the difficulty they experience in understanding social communication and their inability to be flexible (DfES 2002, Munro 2005, Sainsbury 2000).

Kanner and Asperger did not know of each other's work until many years later when Asperger read about Kanner and argued that they had discovered different syndromes. Other academics connected the two. Notably, there was a seminal study in Camberwell in the late 1970s carried out by Judith Gould and Lorna Wing which concluded that autism existed as a spectrum and that its variable symptoms could be diagnosed on a continuum connected by the following features of autistic thinking (Jordan and Powell 1995; 1997, p. 4):

- the way in which information is perceived
- the way the world is experienced
- the way in which information is stored, coded and retrieved from memory
- the way in which emotion interacts with these processes.

Those on the autistic spectrum share symptoms known as the 'triad of impairment' coined in 1981 by Dr Lorna Wing, describing impairment in (Wing 1992):

- social interaction
- social communication
- imaginative thought.

The experience of college

Up until about five years ago, young people with autism or AS who entered FE, having previously attended special schools, may well have found themselves on discrete courses for students with learning disabilities, studying life skills or general courses for vocational preparation despite the fact that they may have had a high IQ. Those who had previously been in mainstream schools may well have had a late diagnosis or, indeed, started college undiagnosed, having spent many previous miserable years in 'D streams' struggling to cope with the social complexities of sharing classrooms with others who were disaffected, disengaged and disruptive. Anecdotal evidence, and my own experience, would suggest that when these young people came to college, it was likely they would have been enrolled on foundation (level 1) courses, often catering or IT, and it would have been rare for them to progress to intermediate or advanced levels. They would leave college and spend many frustrating years doing the rounds of job-centre schemes, locked into long-term unemployment and in social isolation. Many of this 'lost generation' are now returning to FE as adults and can hope that this time their needs will be recognized and met.

Teachers' knowledge, understanding and expertise in dealing with autism and AS has improved significantly over the last five years, largely driven by the rise in inclusive education in primary and secondary schools, combined with improvements in early diagnosis. Specialist training for teachers and changes in resourcing has led to much-improved provisions for pupils with ASD in mainstream schools. Initially, this improvement was in the primary sector (National Autistic Society 2000) and is now being developed in the secondary sector as pupils move through the system (Hesmondhalgh and Breakey 2001). However, good provision is not universal and there are some parents, particularly those of children with more severe symptoms, who believe that mainstream education is wrong for their child and are actively campaigning for special schools to remain open (*The Times* 19 June 2005). FE colleges are currently lagging behind. Good practice is piecemeal and understanding about the support that these students need in order to succeed is still underdeveloped.

When a student with autism or AS applies for a mainstream course in an FE college, he/she may have come from a special school, but it is much more likely that he/she will have come from a mainstream school, which may have been either a positive or negative experience. The student may also have been on a link course and might already know the college, but this will not always be the case. Depending on the central admission and student support services in a college, lecturers may receive comprehensive information about a student with autism or AS. They may also have had some training, but they may have no information, little expertise and not know where to start. If the student is able to discuss their needs, this would indeed make the job easier, but cannot necessarily be expected.

Issues with social communication

Perhaps the most defining characteristic of a person with autism or AS is an inability to manage normal social interaction through which the world is negotiated. This is often under-stood as general social ineptness which manifests itself in a number of ways. Difficulty in understanding and managing social interaction may be evident in an inability to make appropriate eye contact (either not looking at someone or staring at them) and inappropriate or unusual positioning or body posture (usually getting too close). A person with autism or AS tends to hold his/her body tensely, which may be a natural reaction to the tension he/she feels in social situations (Jordan and Powell 1995, p. 57). He/she may lean in to another person's face when they are talking, as if to try to scrutinize their facial expression, which can be interpreted as inap-propriate intimacy or aggression. Emotions tend to be expressed in extremes. Joy may be expressed by leaping up and down rather than through a facial expression such as a smile or a laugh. Anger and frustration may appear inappropriate and extreme. When a 'normal' reaction in a situation might be to get cross or to swear, a student with autism or AS may storm out of a room, slamming a door. This could be in response, for example, to something seemingly innocuous such as a lecturer not having enough handouts or somebody borrowing a pen without asking.

Empathy

Another characteristic of autism or AS is a failure to understand what others think and feel. Jordan and Powell (1999) regard this to be as a result of underdeveloped psychological processes linked to socio-cognition, which leads to what Frith has described as 'mind blindness' and the inability to 'mind read' (Frith 1989, p. 97). In simple terms, having a healthy 'theory of mind' means the ability to judge what another person may be thinking or feeling and to know that these thoughts and feelings might be different from your own. An impaired 'theory of mind' means that the autistic person is unable to empathize and this can have complicated consequences. Smith Myles and Southwick (1999, p. 8) exemplify the profound impact that theory of mind deficit can have and describe the following 'multitude of academic, behaviour and social problems':

- Although those with AS are often highly verbal, they have difficulty explaining why they did something; even when they have a rationale, they cannot give an adequate explanation (for example, why they are late or didn't hand work in).
- Those with AS have only a limited number of emotions and there is little understanding of subtleties; they experience problems in understanding their own state of mind and that of others (for example, they may not recognize that they are anxious or someone else may be embarrassed).
- There are difficulties in understanding another person's perspective in both everyday situations and in relating to historical figures or other famous characters (for example, they may not accept that a lecturer may be too busy or stressed to talk to them).

Baron and Cohen (1993, p. 46) and others (Jordan and Powell 1995) link this 'mind blindness' to an added inability to understand deception and the difference between fact and fiction. On one level, this can leave a person with autism or AS open to potential exploitation. Imagine the minefield of hard-sell advertising, unsolicited junk mail and telephone sales: 'Congratulations, you have won a thousand pounds ... a holiday ... a time-share'. 'Your number has been selected from a million others ...' On another level, it can leave the person with autism or AS vulnerable to genuine frustration. A class-mate says, 'I will see you later' or a lecturer says, 'I will return your marked work next lesson'. In day-to-day reality, these promises are not always delivered and a neuro-typical (non-autistic) person can take this in their stride but an autistic person is more likely to feel very let down or angry and may return to the person involved full of vitriol and indignation. Breaking a promise is seen as totally unacceptable and reasons and excuses will not be heard.

Conversation

To a person with autism or AS, conversation exists primarily as a means of talking about a topic which fascinates him/her. He/she may engage in lengthy monologues on a restricted topic (in stereotypical terms, this has often been exemplified as train timetables, route maps, computer games, film plots and other anorak-type interests, but in reality can be anything). Added to this, a person with autism or AS has a tendency to interpret words and phrases concretely or literally and does not under-stand idiom, irony or sarcasm. This has been wonderfully illustrated by Mark Haddon in his novel, *The Curious Incident of the Dog in the Night-time*, when he describes the confusion for people with autism in interpreting the use of metaphor in everyday language (p. 19):

> 'I laughed my socks off
> The apple of his eye
> They had a skeleton in the cupboard
> We had a real pig of a day
> The dog was stone dead.'

Requests such as: 'Can you close the window?', 'Have you got change of a pound for the drink machine?', 'Have you got a light?' may be answered by yes or no and then followed by a rather blank facial expression and no action, the request having been interpreted literally. 'What's up?' may result in the person looking up at the ceiling to see what's there. In the complex social world of a college, there are so many situations in which a student with autism or AS could find themselves viewed as naive, rude, difficult, belligerent, anti-social or as deliberately 'taking the rise'. They could also be vulnerable to bullying and teasing. Consider the possible trip-wires in these: 'Do you like my jacket?', 'Do you want to come to my place to watch a film?', 'Do I look fat in this?', 'Did you enjoy my lesson?', 'Would you enjoy a trip to ...?', 'What do you think you are playing at?', 'What time do you call this?'

Auditory processing

In addition, people with autism and AS experience great difficulty in taking in information solely through auditory channels. A lecture or a lesson in which the teacher is talking for much of the time can sound like 'white noise' and it is extremely difficult for a person with autism or AS to process what is important and to filter out less important information. This can result in no information having been retained.

Interaction with peers

One of the hallmarks of autism or AS is the difficulty in building and maintaining friendships and other social relationships. As a result, people are frequently isolated or bullied (Smith Myles and Southwick, 1999, p. 14). Asperger offered the reasons for this as:

- an egocentric or self-focused view with little regard for others
- a determination to follow a course of action despite others' concerns
- a tendency to act out (lose their temper or get distressed) when others interfere with their thoughts and actions.

This inability to interact with peers is particularly marked and may mean that the student with autism or AS sits alone in class and often in the same place each week. He/she is likely to find it difficult firstly to select a group and will then find group work or discussion very challenging as a result of his inability to take turns in a conversation or to pick up the threads from other people's views and ideas. He may not see the perspective of another person and will want only to present his own opinion or version of events. Often, in what will appear to be a clumsy attempt to empathize, he will draw on his own past experience in order to make the neurological link in his memory. For example, in a general discussion about the dangers of drugs, he may tell a story of something he has seen in a film or of a time when he was offered drugs. He will not be able to draw generalizations from his experience or to persuade others of his point of view. Indeed, he will not necessarily be clear about his point of view and is more likely to regurgitate facts or repeat the words of others.

A student with autism or AS will not know how to initiate or maintain a conversation or to monitor others' interest or how to interpret the non-verbal clues of interjection. He certainly will not be able to interpret eye rolling or crossed arms (or worse). This may result in him holding the floor or air space for long periods of time (especially if he is interested in the subject), neither anticipating nor inviting interruption. In a class of lively young adults, this can be a recipe for confrontation or aggression from others who judge this behaviour to be egocentric, arrogant and boorish, which will come as a complete surprise to the person with autism or AS. Claire Sainsbury (2002) said:

> 'I was unable to tell whether I was talking too much or to explain to someone why their argument was completely flawed without them becoming offended.'

Rigidity of thought and intolerance of change

Autism and AS are also characterized by ritualistic behaviour, reliance on routines and the absence of imagination (Jordan and Powell 1999, p. 2). This has been linked to an impairment or malfunctioning of the brain's 'executive function', responsible for goal setting, making plans and for managing more than one task at a time. The 'executive function' is vital for making complex choices or decisions, for anticipating the consequence of actions and for understanding cause and effect. Repetitive actions or ritualized behaviour can be seen as a response to loss of this 'higher level executive control' (Frith 1989, p. 179). This can result in an autistic person being locked into self-made routines, which make him or her feel safe, secure and in control. The smallest change in routine can result in high levels of anxiety. Anxiety will then be communicated by anger, withdrawal, obsessive talking, pacing and shouting or, in extreme cases, crying, an upset stomach or sleeplessness. The more anxious the person becomes, the more he or she will need to resort to familiar ritualistic behaviours.

Lack of imagination causes problems in planning or preparing for an event which has not previously been experienced. Spontaneity is a huge threat and is the reason why young people often set up a weekly social routine, i.e. bowling on Monday, swimming Tuesday, etc., which are very hard to deflect from. Despite feeling lonely and isolated, joining in the rather casual and chaotic social life of a college may often be just too hard. However well-managed and planned, colleges are unpredictable places.

Concluding comments

It is crucial that professionals understand the characteristics of ASDs and develop specific skills, foster positive attitudes and provide effective post-compulsory education for students across the spectrum. But it is equally crucial that we remember that students with autism and AS, despite Claire Sainsbury's reference to herself as an 'alien' and Luke Jackson's consideration that he may be a 'freak' and a 'geek' (Jackson 2002), are as individually unique and deserving of equal respect and status as all other students. Richard Exley, who has AS, wrote:

'Individuals (with AS) don't need to be controlled, they need to be respected. They don't need to feel fear or be afraid.

They need the opportunity to be themselves and they need the people around them to give them support to make this happen' (in the introduction to 'Let me in', Hesmondhalgh and Breakey, 2001).

As with any other individual teenager or young adult, students on the autistic spectrum will have their 'meltdowns' and difficult days, but there is evidence to suggest that if stress is reduced, people with AS 'think and feel as others do' (Smith Myles and Southwick 1999, p. 5). This would seem to suggest that if teachers and lecturers, through understanding what is going on, can find ways to reduce the stress for these individuals, the less likely the outbursts, frustration or rigidity.

The following practical suggestions are offered as positive strategies which could help the person with autism or AS and would probably be helpful to many other students, particularly those who have visual and kinaesthetic learning styles and who may have weak auditory processing.

Practical suggestions for managing intolerance of change

- Provide the student with a written timetable.
- Provide the student with a written copy of rules and regulations.
- When unplanned-for change happens, e.g. a lecturer is off sick and a class is cancelled, if at all possible give the student advance notice in writing or a text message about what is going to happen.
- When a trip is planned, take time to talk the student through the sequence of events, deal with questions and anxieties and provide back-up information in written form.

Practical suggestions for communication

- Devote some tutorial session to explaining autism and AS to the group, allowing maximum negotiation and involvement of the student with ASD.

- Keep verbal communication minimum and provide key instructions and information in written form (task sheets).
- Use visual clues and reminders wherever possible, even if the student is highly articulate (frequent use of the whiteboard, handouts, etc.).
- Avoid language where meaning must be inferred, for example, say: 'Please put your bag on the floor' rather than 'Have you got enough room with that bag on the table?'
- Avoid open-ended questions.
- Tell the student why the information is useful, how he or she can use it and where it fits in with the knowledge he or she already possesses.
- Present the lesson components visually (a lesson sequence with timings or a lesson 'mind map' on a flip chart or whiteboard).
- Tick these components off as the lesson progresses.
- Deliver complex information in increments.
- Use modelling and demonstration to show a student what to do or how to approach and complete a task.
- Deliver new material more than once.
- Consider paired work or buddying to help the student stay on task *or* allow the student to remove him/herself from the group and sit with his/her back to the others on his own table to reduce noise and visual distraction (he/she will know which he prefers).

Practical suggestions for group work

- Place the student with autism or AS in a group with classmates who are calmer and more mature.
- Teach group discussion skills and set rules for turn-taking.
- Consider alternative cues for interruption or changing the topic that are easy to interpret, i.e. holding up coloured cards – orange means 'I want to interrupt', red means the other person has gone on too long and green means 'I want to change the topic'.
- Monitor the interactions and reactions of the person with

autism or AS and ensure that they are included or not distressed – join the group if necessary.

- Respond positively to his contributions as a model to the other students.
- Help him/her to make the generalizations and connections from his own experience using clear statements or questions. For example, in a general discussion about drugs: 'Do you think it was right or wrong that someone offered the character in the film drugs?', 'Why do you think they did it?', 'Why was it wrong?'
- After the class, debrief the student and give feedback specifically about what was successful in terms of his or her interaction and what didn't work.

To conclude, Claire Sainsbury, taken from her book *Martian in the Playground*:

'Schoolchildren with Asperger's syndrome are not the easiest pupils to have in one's class and even those who are sympathetic to us find us baffling and even infuriating at times. Nevertheless I hope I can say without boasting that we must be among the most interesting and challenging students that a teacher will ever encounter. We also offer teachers that rare thing: the chance to make a real difference. One point that stood out from many different stories was that the presence of even one teacher who was willing to approach a student with Asperger's with insight and respect could make a dramatic difference to the whole school career and even life as a whole, even though that student may not have been able to express their gratitude or provide any positive feedback at the time. Conversely, ignorance and intolerance could scar a child for life' (2000, p. 130).

Conclusion

Now that you have read about a variety of ways in which you can practise differentiation within your own classroom, let us return to the central concept of this book – inclusion, which was defined in the first chapter.

We hope this book has increased your confidence in responding to various individual needs, but also that it has given you a new insight into the concept of inclusion itself. In the view of the authors inclusion is not something which is finite and simply able to be ticked off like a performance indicator; rather it is a goal towards which committed teachers are continuously striving. Inclusion is a practical philosophy, guided by an underlying commitment to each individual's inalienable rights, by virtue of being human, to social justice and equity. It is an aspiration towards which we are constantly working and a practice which demands energy and commitment.

Another book in this series, *Ultimate FE Leadership and Management Handbook* (Jameson and McNay), reminds us that good leadership and management puts the individual learner at the centre of education and this is, after all, what inclusion aims to achieve. This notion of welcoming all learners, regardless of background and ability, has always been characteristic of further education. Inclusion lies at the heart of further education and has historically distinguished it from school and higher education sectors, both of which have been driven by, and perpetuated by, selection.

In recent years reforms have been designed to focus further education colleges into competitive corporations driven by market forces, profits and a business ideology. Despite this some institutions have remained loyal to the founding principles of 'second chance' learning and extended opportunities to those disadvantaged and excluded by sectors that perpetuate stratification by social class and privilege. These colleges, which embed diversity and inclusion within the fabric of their institution, lead the way and remind us of those core values of inclusion which are fundamental to post compulsory education.

At the time of writing, those of us who observe with a critical eye question whether government initiatives such as in 'Success for All' and 'Skills for Life', which appear to endorse the philosophy of inclusion and uphold values of equal opportunities are actually driven by functionalist, utilitarian values. If this is the case rhetoric may seduce the sector into believing that when attainment targets alone are met, we are succeeding in serving the needs of our learners.

This is not to argue that achievement measured by qualification is unimportant. Qualifications matter but they are not the sole indicator of educational success. Successful learning is often life enhancing in ways which cannot be quantified, weighed, measured and turned into a single recipe for all. Inclusive cultures will inevitably be a challenge in the current climate, but it is the hope of the authors that what we have shared with you will help you to promote and defend learning that affirms less conventional abilities and diverse achievements and celebrates the richness of difference.

References

Ainscow, M. (1997) 'Towards inclusive schooling' in *British Journal of Special Education*, vol. 24, no. 1.

Anderson, V., Farraday, S., Prowne, S., Richards, G. and Swindells, D. (2003) *Count Me in FE*. London: Learning and Skills Development Agency.

Armitage, A. and Bryant, R. (eds) (2001) *Teaching in Post-compulsory Education*. Buckingham: Open University Press.

Baker, C. (2002) *Foundations of Bilingual Education and Bilingualism*. Clevedon: Multilingual Matters.

Barnes, C. (1996) 'Theories of disability and the origins of the oppression of disabled people in Western society' in Barton, L. (ed.) *Disability and Society: Emerging issues and insights*. Harlow: Longman.

Baron-Cohen, S. and Bolton, P. (1993) *Autism: The facts*. New York: Oxford University Press.

Barton, L. 1988 (ed.) *The Politics of Special Educational Needs*. Lewis: Routledge Falmer.

Bigge, M. and Shermis, S. (1982) *Learning Theories for Teachers*. London: Harper and Rowe.

Block, D. (2003) *The Social Turn in Second Language Acquisition*. Edinburgh: Edinburgh University Press.

Bolloten, B. and Spafford, T. (1998) *Teaching Refugee Students*. Stoke on Trent: Trentham Books.

Bourne, J. and McPake, J. (1991) *Partnership Teaching*. London: HMSO.

Brennan, Zoe (2005) 'Education: Solving the special needs school crisis' in *The Times*, 19 June 2005.

Brewin, M. and Demetriades, A. (1998) *Raising the Profile of Invisible Students*. London: Children of the Storm.

Centre for Studies in Inclusive Education (2001) 'Index for Inclusion: Developing learning and participation in schools' in *School Change Through Inclusion*, www.csie.org.uk. Last accessed: July 2005.

Clark, C., Dyson, A. and Millward, A. (eds) (1998) *Theorising Special Education*. London and New York: Routledge.

Clarke, C. and Millward, A. (1995) *Towards Inclusive Schools*. London: David Fulton.

Commission for Racial Equality (2005), http://cre.gov.uk. Last accessed: January 2006.

Cook, V. (1998) *Chomsky's Universal Grammar*. Oxford: Blackwell.

Corbett, J. (1996) *Bad Mouthing: The language of special needs*. London: Cassell.

Corbett, J. and Slee, R. (2000) 'An international conversation on inclusive education' in Armstrong, F., Armstrong, D. and Barton, L. (eds) *Inclusive Education: Policy, contexts and comparative perspectives*. London: David Foulton.

Coren, A. (1997) A *Psychodynamic Approach to Education*. London: Sheldon Press.

Critchley, M. (1970) *The Dyslexic Child*. Springfield: Charles Thomas.

Department for Education and Employment (1999a) *A Fresh Start – Improving Literacy and Numeracy: The report of the working group chaired by Sir Claus Moser*. London: DfEE.

Department for Education and Employment (1999) 'Learning to succeed: A new framework for post-16 learning'. London: The Stationary Office.

Department for Education and Skills (2001) 'Inclusive schooling children with special educational needs guidance' (November DfES/0774/2001) London: DfES.

Department for Education and Skills (2002) 'Autistic spectrum disorders: A good practice guide' (DfES 597/2002/REV). Nottingham: DfES.

Department for Education and Skills (2003) 'Skills for life: Focus on delivery to 2007'. London: DfES.

Department for Education and Skills (2005) 'Gender and achievement', www.standards.dfes.gov.uk/genderandachievement. Last accessed: January 2006.

Ellis, R. (1997) *Second Language Acquisition*. Oxford: Oxford University Press.

Equal Opportunities Commission (2005b) 'Action for change', www.eoc.org.uk. Last accessed: January 2006.

Equal Opportunities Commission (2005a) 'Facts about women and men in Great Britain', www.eoc.org.uk. Last accessed: January 2006.

European Parliament (2005) 'Facts about women and men in Great Britain', www.eoc.org.uk. Last accessed: January 2006.

Farrell, P. (2000) *The Management, Training and Roles of LSAs*. London: David Fulton.

Farrell, P. (2001) 'Special education in the last twenty years: Have things really got better?' *British Journal of Special Education*, vol. 28, no. 1.

Farrell, P. and Ainscow, M. (2003) *Making Special Education Inclusive.* London: David Fulton.

Fawcett, A. J. and Nicolson, R. L. (1992) 'Automatisation deficits in balance for dyslexic children: Perceptual and motor skills' in JOURNAL NAME?, vol. 75 no. 2, pp. 507–29.

Fox, G. (2003) *A Handbook for Learning Support Assistants.* London: David Fulton.

Freeman, K. (1977) *The Invisible Students: Refugees and further education.* Birmingham: National Extension College.

Frith, U. (1989) *Autism: Explaining the enigma.* Oxford: Blackwell.

Further Education Development Agency (1998) *Inclusive Colleges: Building on inclusive practice,* no. 2. Available in the FEDA archives at: www.lsda.org.uk. Last accessed: ??

Galaburda, A. and Kemper, T. (1979) 'Cytoarchitectonic abnormalities in developmental dyslexia: A case study' in *Annal of Neurology,* vol. 6, pp. 94–100.

General Register Office for Scotland (2004) *Scotland's Census 2001* in Equal Opportunities Commission, 'Facts about women and men in Great Britain', www.eoc.org.uk. Last accessed: January 2006.

Green, P. (1999) *Raise the standard: A practical guide to raising ethnic minority and bilingual pupils' achievement.* Stoke on Trent: Trentham Books.

Haddon, Mark (2003) *The Curious Incident of the Dog in the Night-time.* London: Jonathan Cape.

Hamilton, R. and Moore, D. (2003) *Educational Interventions for Refugee Children: Theoretical perspectives and implementing best practice.* London: Routledge Falmer.

Harkin J. (2002) 'Constructs used by 17–19-year-old students in Northern Europe when informally evaluating their teachers' in *Educational Research Journal,* vol. 1, no. 3.

Hesmondhalgh, M. and Breakey, C. (2001) *Access and Inclusion for Children with Autistic Spectrum Disorders.* London: Jessica Kingsley.

House of Commons (2004) 'Weekly information bulletin', 18 December 2004.

Jackson, L. (2002) *Freaks, Geeks and Asperger's Syndrome: A guide to adolescence.* London: Jessica Kingsley.

Jordan, R. and Powell, S. (1995) *Understanding and Teaching Children with Autism.* Chichester: Wiley.

Kanner, L. and Eisenberg, L. (1956) 'Early infantile autism' in *American Journal of Orthopsychiatry,* pp. 1943–55.

Katzner, K. (1999) *Languages of the World.* London: Routledge.

Kershaw, R. and Pearsall, M. (2000) *Immigrants and Aliens: A guide to sources on UK immigration and citizenship.* London: The National Archives.

Klein, C. (1997) *Diagnosing Dyslexia*. London: Basic Skills Agency.

Knox, K. (1997) *Credit to the Nation: A study of refugees in the United Kingdom*. London: The Refugee Council.

Learning and Skills Development Agency (2002) *Access for All*. London: DfES.

Learning and Skills Development Agency and Oxford Brookes University (2004) 'Meeting the needs of younger learners in further education' in *The Times Educational Supplement*, 26 November 2004.

Learning Skills Council (2004) 'Further education, work-based learning for young people and adult and community learning – learner numbers in England' in Equal Opportunities Commission (2005) 'Facts about women and men in Great Britain', www.eoc.org.uk. Last accessed: January 2006.

Ledoux, J. (1998) *The Emotional Brain*. London: Phoenix.

Leiner, H. C., Leiner, A. C. and Dow, R. S. (1991) 'The human cerebro-cerebellar system: Its computing, cognitive and language skills' in *Behavioural Brain Research*, vol. 44, pp. 113–28.

Levinson, H. (2003) *Smart But Feeling Dumb*. New York: Warner Books.

Llinas R. and Solelo, C. (1992) *The Cerebellum Revisted*. New York: Springer-Verlag.

Lunt, I. and Norwich, B. (1999). 'Perspectives on Educational Policy' in *Can Effective Schools be Inclusive Schools?* London: Institute of Education, University of London.

Medical Review Council (2001) 'Review of autism research: Epidemiology and causes', www.mrc.ac/pdf.autism-report. Last accessed:?.

Mitchell, R. and Myles, F. (1998) *Second Language Learning Theories*. London: Hodder Arnold.

Mittler, P. (2000) *Working Towards Inclusive Education: Social contexts*. London: David Foulton.

Morris, B. (1991) 'The nature and role of educational therapy' in *Journal of Educational Therapy*, vol. 3, no. 3.

Munrow, N. (2005) 'What is the difference between high-functioning autism and Asperger Syndrome?', www.nas.org.uk. Last accessed: 23 July 2005

National Autistic Society (2000) 'Inclusion and autism: Is it working?' London: National Autistic Society.

National Autistic Society (2001) 'Ignored or intelligible: The reality for adults with autism spectrum disorders'. London: National Autistic Society.

Nayar, J. (2004) 'A study of an individual's languages and literacies' in *Language Issues*, vol. 16, no.2.

Office of National Statistics (2004a) 'Annual survey of hours and earnings' in Equal Opportunities Commission (2005) 'Facts about women and men in Great Britain', www.eoc.org.uk. Last accessed: January 2006.

Office of National Statistics (2004b) 'Census 2001: National report for England and Wales' in Equal Opportunities Commission 'Facts about women and men in Great Britain', www.eoc.org.uk. Last accessed January 2006.

Office of National Statistics (2004c) 'Labour force survey' in Equal Opportunities Commission (2005) 'Facts about women and men in Great Britain', www.eoc.org.uk. Last accessed: January 2006.

Ofsted (2000) 'Evaluating educational inclusion'. London: Ofsted.

Ofsted (2004) 'Why colleges succeed'. London: Ofsted.

Ofsted (2005) *The Handbook for Inspecting Colleges*. London: Ofsted.

Oliver, M. (1988) 'The social and political context of educational policy: the case of special needs' in Barton, L. (ed.) *The Politics of Special Educational Needs*. Lewis: Falmer.

Oliver, M. (1995) 'Does special education have a role to play in the 21st century?' in *REACH Journal of Special Educational Needs in Ireland*, vol. 8, no. 2.

Orton, S. (1937) TITLE?, www.clubi.ie/dyslexia. Last accessed:?

Piatelli-Palmarini, M. (ed.) (1980) *Language and Learning: The debate between Jean Piaget and Noam Chomsky*. London: Routledge and Kegan Paul.

Powell, J. and Jordan, R. (eds) (1997) 'Propositions underlying our understanding of autism' in *Autism and Learning A Guide to Good Practice*. London: David Fulton.

Powell, S. and Jordan, R. (eds) (1997) *Autism and Learning: A guide to good practice*. London: David Fulton.

Power, S., Whitty, G. and Youdell, D. (1998) 'Refugees, asylum seekers and the housing crisis: No place to learn' in Jones, C. and Rutter, J. (eds) *Refugee Education: Mapping the field*, Stoke on Trent: Trentham Books.

Prosser, M. (2005) 'The big pay back' in the *Guardian*, 7 September 2005.

Rogers, C. (1951) *Client-centred Therapy: Its current practice, implications and theory*. Boston: Houghton Mifflin.

Rutter, J. and Jones, C. (eds) (1998) *Refugee Education: Mapping the field*. Stoke on Trent: Trentham Books.

Sainsbury, C. (2000) *Martian in the Playground*. London: The Book Factory.

Salzberger-Wittenberg, I., Henry, G. and Osborne, E. (1983) *The Emotional Experience of Learning and Teaching*. London: Routledge.

Senior, J. (2002) 'Asylum seekers: who cares?' in *The Psychologist*, vol. 15, no. 8 pp. 392–3.

Slater, J. (2004) 'Special needs strategy in trouble' in *The Times Educational Supplement*, 13 February 2004.

Smith, F. 'Quotations on teaching, learning and education', www.ntlf.com/html/lib/quotes.htm. Last accessed: November 2005.

Smith Myles, B. and Southwick, J. (1999) *Asperger's Syndrome and the Difficult Moments*. Kansas: Autism Asperger's Publishing Company.

Smyth, G. (2003) *Helping Bilingual Pupils to Access the Curriculum*. London: David Fulton.

Speare, J. (2004) 'FE teachers' quotations', unpublished interviews.

Swain, M. (1972) 'Bilingualism as First Language', unpublished PhD dissertation, University of California Irvine, cited in Nayar, J. (2004) 'A study of an individual's languages and literacies' in *Language Issues*, vol. 16, no. 2.

Target, F. (2003) *Working in English Language Teaching* (2nd edn). London: Kogan Page.

Tawney, A. H. (1964) *Equality*. London: George Allen and Unwin.

Thomas, G. (1992) *Effective Classroom Teamwork: Support or intrusion?* London: Routledge.

Thomas, G. and Loxley, A. (2001) *Deconstructing Special Education and Reconstructing Inclusion*. Buckingham: Open University Press.

Thomas, G. and Vaughan, M. (2004) *Inclusive Education Readings and Reflections*. Buckingham: Open University Press.

Tomlinson, J. (1996) *Inclusive Learning – Principals and Recommendations. A summary of the findings of the learning difficulties and disabilities committee.* Coventry: FEFC

Tomlinson, S. (2001) *Education in a Post-welfare Society*. Buckingham: Open University Press.

Tuckman, B. (1965) 'Developmental sequences in small groups' in *Psychological Bulletin*, vol. 63, pp. 384–99.

UNESCO (1994) *World Conference on Special Needs Education: Access and quality*. Paris: UNESCO

Visser, J. and Upton, G. (1993) *Special Education in Britain after Warnock*. London: David Fulton.

Vygotsky, L. S. (1962) *Thought and Language*. Cambridge, MA: MIT Press.

Ware, L. (1995) 'The aftermath of the articulate debate: The invention of inclusive education' in Clarke, C., Dyson, A. and Millward, A. (eds) *Towards Inclusive Schooling*. London: David Fulton.

Warnock, M. (1978) 'Special educational needs: Report of the committee of enquiry into the education of handicapped children and young people'. London: HMSO.

Whitty, G. (2002) *Making Sense of Educational Policy*. London: Paul Chapman.

Wing, L. (1992) *Autistic Spectrum Disorders: An aid to diagnosis* (3rd edn.) London: National Autistic Society.

World Health Organisation (1992) *International Classification of Diseases* (10th edn) in Smith Myles, B. and Southwick, J. (1999) *Asperger's Syndrome and the Difficult Moments*. Kansas: Autism Asperger's Publishing Company.

Wright, A. M. (2006) 'Students with severe learning difficulties in general colleges of further education: Have we been going round in circles?' in *British Journal of Special Education*, vol. 33, no. 1.

Index